Ex. 11/06 No further eds. 1©
624.1771HAN
(D22)

Principles of Structures

Ariel Hanaor

National Building Research Institute
The Technion, Israel Institute of Technology

b

**Blackwell
Science**

© Ariel Hanaor 1998
Blackwell Science Ltd
Editorial Offices:
Osney Mead, Oxford OX2 0EL
25 John Street, London WC1N 2BL
23 Ainslie Place, Edinburgh EH3 6AJ
350 Main Street, Malden
  MA 02148 5018, USA
54 University Street, Carlton
  Victoria 3053, Australia
10, rue Casimir Delavigne
  75006 Paris, France

Other Editorial Offices:

Blackwell Wissenschafts-Verlag GmbH
Kurfürstendamm 57
10707 Berlin, Germany

Blackwell Science KK
MG Kodenmacho Building
7–10 Kodenmacho Nihombashi
Chuo-ku, Tokyo 104, Japan

First published 1998

Set in 10/13 pt Times
by Aarontype Limited, Bristol
Printed and bound in Great Britain by
the University Press, Cambridge

DISTRIBUTORS
Marston Book Services Ltd
PO Box 269
Abingdon
Oxon OX14 4YN
(*Orders*: Tel: 01235 465500
          Fax: 01235 465555)

USA
Blackwell Science, Inc.
Commerce Place
350 Main Street
Malden, MA 02148 5018
(*Orders*: Tel: 800 759 6102
                  781 388 8250
          Fax: 781 388 8255)

Canada
  Login Brothers Book Company
  324 Saulteaux Crescent
  Winnipeg, Manitoba R3J 3T2
  (*Orders*: Tel: 204 224-4068)

Australia
  Blackwell Science Pty Ltd
  54 University Street
  Carlton, Victoria 3053
  (*Orders*: Tel: 03 9347 0300
            Fax: 03 9347 5001)

A catalogue record for this title
is available from the British Library

ISBN 0-632-04262-1

Library of Congress
Cataloging-in-Publication Data

Hanaor, Ariel.
    Principles of structures/Ariel Hanaor.
      p. cm.
    Includes bibliographical references and index.
    ISBN 0-632-04262-1 (pbk.)
    1. Structural design.   I. Title.
TA658.H36   1998
624.1'771–dc21   98-12769
                                                      CIP

In memory of my father

Everything that can be expressed in words can be expressed clearly.

(Alles was sich aussprechen läßt, läßt sich klar aussprechen.)

What cannot be expressed in words must remain unuttered.

(Wovon man nicht sprechen kann, darüber muß man schweigen.)

Ludwig Wittgenstein, *Tractatus Logico-Philosophicus (Logisch-philosophische Abhandlung)*

Contents

Preface

The idea for this book sprang from an introductory course on the 'Theory of Structures' to first year architecture students. As an experienced structural engineer, I was faced with the daunting task of attempting to give an audience, with practically no scientific background to speak of, a fundamental understanding (be it at the conceptual level only) of some very sophisticated concepts – a sort of bird's eye view of the whole of structural engineering. The problem consisted of clarifying these concepts at basic high-school level, without on one hand resorting to jargon and extensive mathematical formulation or, on the other hand, trivialising the issues involved and obscuring their complexities.

It turned out to be an extremely intense intellectual effort. I quickly came to realise the extent to which practising professionals tend to take for granted immanently complex concepts, such as *force*, *equilibrium*, *stability*, *stiffness/flexibility* etc. By studying these concepts from the bottom up, as it were, we have lost perspective of their fundamental meaning and significance, free of the trappings of mathematical formulation, computational complexities and design codes. The considerable effort involved in trying to get free of these trappings, and reveal the essential, fundamental significance of the concepts which govern the behaviour of structures, and how and why they do so, is extremely rewarding, not just as an intellectual exercise, but perhaps more importantly, as a very powerful design tool. The depth and breadth of understanding gained by this approach enables the designer to concentrate on the essential in structural design, and to exploit this understanding in devising better, sometimes new, structural solutions to the problem at hand.

The book is, therefore, aimed primarily at students beginning architecture and engineering courses. It attempts to give the novice an overview of the field of structural engineering and design, providing a sort of mental map to help students navigate, as they penetrate deeper into the ever increasing complexities and intricacies of the field. It is hoped that experienced professionals may also find the book of interest, helping them to break free of these intricacies and complexities and 'clear the drawing board', as it were, for a fresh look at what structural engineering is essentially about. It is not intended as a textbook. Design (see Chapter 1) cannot be learned from a text, as a body of knowledge that needs to be assimilated. Design can only be learned through the practice of design. Books such as this can only serve as assistance and stimulus for the creative process of design, and as a sort of 'lexicon' for a basic vocabulary which enables communication among practitioners.

The book relates primarily to the conceptual design of structures. However, with the exception of the first chapter, very little direct reference to design issues is made. The first, introductory chapter is a general outline of the design process, aimed primarily at the novice. Design, like any creative process, is a highly subjective and individualistic activity. Experienced designers will have formed their own approach and views, and any pronouncement on this subject is bound to be controversial. For the novice, however, it is important to develop sound, rational design methodologies, based on understanding of the basic principles governing the designed object. Intuition can be a powerful design tool for the experienced designer who has assimilated these principles, but a very treacherous approach for the novice. It is with this view that the first chapter is written. The remainder of the book deals with those fundamental concepts and principles which should form the basis for a rational structural design.

The book consists of two major parts. The first part introduces the basic concepts essential to the understanding of structural behaviour. The second part is a survey of structural systems and their main structural features. The two parts are quite independent, enabling access to structural systems without a thorough study of basic concepts (e.g. by persons familiar with these concepts). Although the second part employs concepts and terms introduced in the first part, direct reference can be made to the definitions of these concepts through the index at the end of the book.

The driving force behind this work and the format incorporating it is the striving for clarity and simplicity. The presentation is crisp and concise, attempting to **demonstrate** as much as possible, rather than spell out the various topics. The format adopted in an attempt to implement this goal is as follows:

0.0.1   Concepts are presented in short, sequentially numbered sections, such as this one, for easy reference (through the index). The statements say just what is essential for understanding, leaving demonstration and some elaboration to the illustrations.

0.0.2   The material is presented in separate columns of text and illustrations. In this way the text flows unbroken, while allowing easy reference to the illustrations which complement it. Both text and illustrations are essential to the understanding of the material. The illustrations **show** those things which cannot be clearly expressed in words (see motto).

0.0.3   *Keywords* appear in bold italics where they are first defined or explained. *Keywords* appearing before they are defined are in plain italics (to identify them as keywords). Definitions are intended to be com-prehensible and as accurate as possible, within the context and framework of the book. They are not intended to be general, comprehensive or scientifically rigorous. Clarity often takes precedence over rigour, provided no fundamental principle is distorted, ignored or glossed over.

Unnumbered clauses set out thus in a different font contain further elaboration, explanation or in depth analysis, which go beyond the general intended scope of the book and can be skipped without loss of continuity or of essential information.

The central theme of the book is the close link between form and structure, between geometry and the flow of forces in the structure. This link finds its expression most succinctly in the fundamental concept of *Structural depth*. In the whole book, there is practically no direct reference to 'aesthetics', its central role in architecture notwithstanding. The deliberate avoidance of this term is part of the attempt at clarity and simplicity mentioned above, 'aesthetics' (or 'beauty') being one of those things which, according to Wittgenstein, cannot be expressed in words, and therefore cannot be expressed clearly. There is, however, an attempt to **show** that true expression of the relation between form and structure is an aesthetic principle, without attempting to evaluate the importance of this principle.

The bulk of the illustrations were painstakingly hand drawn by Bernardo (Ben) Katz.

I thank my friend and colleague Professor Abraham (Fredi) Ben-Arroyo, without whose inspiration and encouragement this book would not have been written.

Ariel Hanaor

Part I Basic Concepts

1 Introduction: The Design Process

1.1 Design

Design

A process of *synthesis* of an 'object' (a product, building, city etc.) from given data, by employing Design tools and Design criteria and subject to Constraints.

Object

The process, like any human activity, and particularly a creative one, is extremely complex. The discussion that follows is an attempt to outline the essentials of the process in as objective manner as possible. A step by step description of the process is given below. The process is applicable to the design of any object. Considerations related specifically to the design of structures are surveyed in following chapters.

1.1.1 Synthesis

Synthesis

A process in which an object is assembled, created or generated, from basic components or data. A problem in synthesis typically has multiple solutions.

1.1.2 Analysis

Analysis

A process of disassembling or dissecting an existing entity (object, phenomenon, idea etc.) into its basic components. A problem in analysis typically has a single solution (although the solution may consist of several parts).

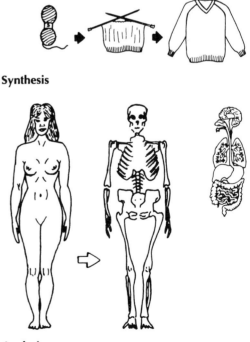

Synthesis

Analysis

1.1.3 Theory

Theory
An analytical framework providing a systematic description of a system or class of existing entities ('structures' in the present context).

1.2 Design tools

Design tools
The means employed in the design process. The main tools, in order of significance and precedence are:

- ❑ 'Blank page' (see design step 1 – 1.4.1 below).
- ❑ Common sense.
- ❑ Experience (gained through the practice of design).
- ❑ Theory.
- ❑ Design codes (Chapter 2).
- ❑ Design aids, such as design guides, product catalogues, computer programs (e.g. CAD).

1.3 Types of design

The design of a large object, such as a building, typically consists of the three phases listed below. The process is general for the design of any product, but a building or another type of structure is used as a model.

1.3.1 Conceptual design

Conceptual design
A design phase beginning with the initial data (the 'brief') and ending with a number of concepts for the 'product'. For example, when the 'product' being designed is a building, the results of the conceptual design may include such features as the general shape, layout of spaces, and the types of the main supporting elements of the structure and their locations, without details or accurate

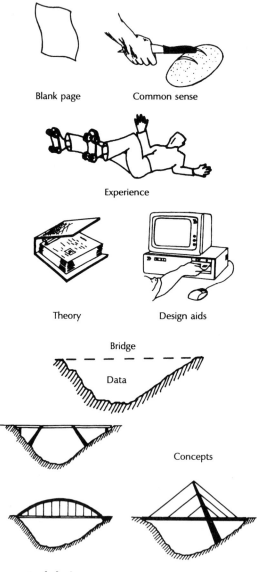

Blank page   Common sense

Experience

Theory   Design aids

Concepts

Conceptual design

dimensions. The design tools which feature most prominently in conceptual design are the three listed first in 1.2 (blank page, common sense, experience).

1.3.2 Preliminary design

Preliminary design
A design phase beginning with the concepts developed in the conceptual phase and ending with fewer variants (usually one or two), including approximate sizes and rough details.

Preliminary design

1.3.3 Final design

Final design
The final design phase, starting with the preliminary design of the selected variant, and ending with the working drawings, shop drawings and other project documents.

The design tools featuring in preliminary and final design are mainly the last three listed in 1.2 (theory, codes and design aids), but common sense and experience play an overriding role. The present work is concerned mainly with conceptual design.

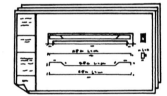

Drawings

Final design

1.4 The design process step by step

1.4.1 Preliminaries

1.4.1.1 Step 1
Blank page

Empty the mind of any preconceived ideas, intuition, prior experience (e.g. of similar projects). It is important to embark on a new project with a fresh outlook. This is probably the most important step and the hardest to accomplish. Experience and intuition will play their role willy nilly, but it is important to rein them in and subject them to the *constraints* of the problem at hand (see below).

Design example

Chair

Open mind

Blank page

1.4.1.2 Step 2
Presentation of the data and design objectives

The data as initially given is usually incomplete and not well defined. Important items are often obscured by marginal details. At this stage the data is sorted systematically, and presented in a way that clearly defines the main problems to be solved. In particular, the main objectives and secondary objectives are defined, as are the *Constraints* and requirements.

Constraint
A condition imposed on the designed object. The constraint can be imposed explicitly, as part of the data, or be implied by the nature of the designed object or the data.

> For example: a chair has to possess dimensions and shape enabling sitting down and getting up, comfort, support, etc. Different types of chairs have different constraints relating to their function (armchair, office chair etc.).

The designed object has to satisfy all the constraints without exception. All data, including all the constraints, constitute the design problem. Altering a data item or a constraint implies altering the problem, requiring the design process to be restarted.

1.4.1.3 Step 3
Analysis of the data and the constraints

The significance of the data and constraints is assessed and implications drawn, often producing further constraints (e.g. on materials, colours etc.).

1.4.2 Design activity: the Design Tree

1.4.2.1 Step 4
Generation of design alternatives

A successful design cannot be based on a single conceptual variant 'plucked out of the blue', or based on intuition alone. A good design is the result of careful selection between alternatives.

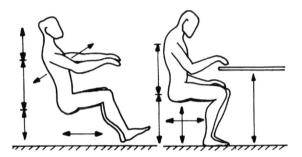

Dimensions, constraints

'Art lives by constraints and dies of freedom'

Leonardo da Vinci

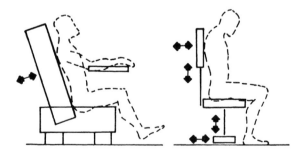

Functional requirements

The development of design alternatives is based on the fact that any design problem (as distinguished from analysis problem) has many solutions, and every solution produces new problems.

The process can be summarised as follows:

❏ Based on the data and the constraints, formulate **at least two** substantially different general concepts (see 'Conceptual design' above). To follow the chair example, two possibilities could be a soft padded chair or a solid (e.g. wooden) one.

❏ Each of the solutions will generate its own problems, for example the material for the framework of the chair. Provide at least two, substantially different, solutions for each problem. For example metal frame or wooden frame, sponge padding or elastic membrane, etc.

❏ Repeat the process until a sufficient number of conceptually distinct alternatives are obtained. The process is a geometric progression and a large number of alternatives is quickly produced. What is a 'sufficient' number will depend on the scale of the project, and on the inclination of the designer, but a rough guide for conceptual design of, say, a building, is between four and eight alternatives.

1.4.2.2 Step 5

Definition of design criteria

This step can be performed at any stage after step 1 but it is presented here, at the stage when *Design criteria* are needed to compare alternatives.

Design criterion

A measure of some aspect of the quality of a proposed design solution. For example, the comfort of the chair, its durability, colour fastness, ease of sitting and getting up, weight, **cost** etc., can all serve as design criteria in the chair example.

It is important to distinguish between a design criterion and a constraint. As mentioned above, a solution which violates any constraint is not in

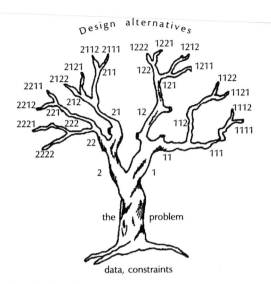

The design tree

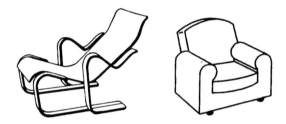

Design alternatives

fact a solution to the given problem, and either the solution is rejected or the problem is redefined. On the other hand a design criterion can be satisfied to a greater or lesser extent.

In the literature the term design criterion is sometimes attached to pass/fail tests such as code requirements (e.g. strength or serviceability requirements). These are in fact constraints and not criteria, since any solution violating them cannot be considered at all.

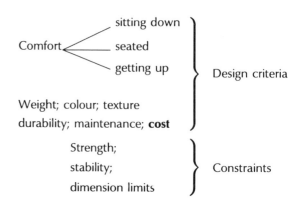

1.4.2.3 Step 6
Comparison of design alternatives

The comparison can be qualitative or quantitative to varying degrees, but even in an apparently quantitative analysis the assigning of weights to different criteria, and the assignment of marks to solutions, are based on the designer's judgment and are highly subjective.

Nevertheless, the designer must resist, as far as possible, the temptation to assign weights so as to arrive at a favourite preselected choice. An honest, even-handed selection process can sometimes lead to unexpected and gratifying results.

1.4.2.4 Step 7
Selection and update

The selection is based on the comparison of step 6, but subject to the designer's judgment.

The number of selected alternatives for the next phase of the design depends on the size of the project and the nature of the next phase. In the case of conceptual design at least two alternatives will usually be selected for preliminary design, more in a large project. It is rare for more than one alternative to be considered in the final design phase.

On the basis of the comparison, it is sometimes possible to improve a selected solution, in categories indicated by the design criteria, prior to moving to the next stage. For instance, it may be

Alt No	Design criteria (marks of 10) (· · ·) weight				Final mark (weighted sum)
	1 (1)	2 (3)	3 (1)		
1	5	8	7		36
2	8	5	8		31
⋮					

possible to reduce the weight of the chair (the structure) without making it too weak.

1.4.2.5 Step 8
Updating

Return to step 6, in the case where updating has been carried out in the preceding step. This is not usually applicable to the conceptual phase since it involves refinement rather than change of concept.

1.4.3 Post processing (output)

1.4.3.1 Step 9
Presentation of results

Production of models, drawings, prototypes, etc. according to the nature of the project and the design phase (1.3).

1.4.3.2 Step 10
Proceed to next phase

From conceptual design proceed to preliminary design or from preliminary to final design.

1.5 Some general comments

❑ The selection between design alternatives should be put off as late as possible, in order to avoid the natural inclination for prejudged preferences.

❑ Design often has to do with shape or form (architectural design, product design, structural design etc.). In design (as distinct from styling) shape (geometry) is, in most cases, the result (output) of the design, not an input (data, constraint or criterion).

❑ The relationship between the shape of a structure and the principles governing its behaviour is the central theme of this work. Presuming a shape amounts to dictating a mode of behaviour, which, unless the presumption is based on thorough structural knowledge, is likely to produce poor results.

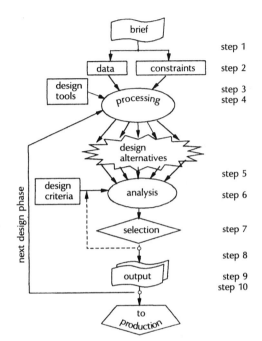

The design process

'Inspiration is a result of concentrated effort'

2 Structure

Structure

That part of the object (building, bridge, chair, living body etc.) which is responsible for maintaining the **shape** of the object under the **influence of the environment**.

2.1 Forces and loads

The influence of the environment on structures takes the form, principally, of *Loads* and *Forces*. Here the word 'environment' is taken to mean anything in contact with the structure (e.g. vehicles, furniture, people etc.), including the structure itself. Such primary environmental influences as wind, temperature, earthquake affect the structure by exerting forces on it. The remainder of the chapter is concerned chiefly with these concepts.

2.1.1 Force

Force

Influence on a body, causing (or attempting to cause) the *Movement* of the body or part of it, or causing a change in its movement, if it is already in motion.

> This is the common definition of force encountered in the literature. It is interesting to note that even though force is one of the most fundamental concepts in physics, its definition is indirect, relying on its effect. This is an indication of the complexity of this concept and the difficulty in visualising it.

The definition of force through the concept of motion, a concept which is easy to grasp intuitively, enables easy visualisation of forces, and brings forth the extremely important relationship between force and motion. This, in fact, is the source of the force–shape relationship which is the focal point of this work.

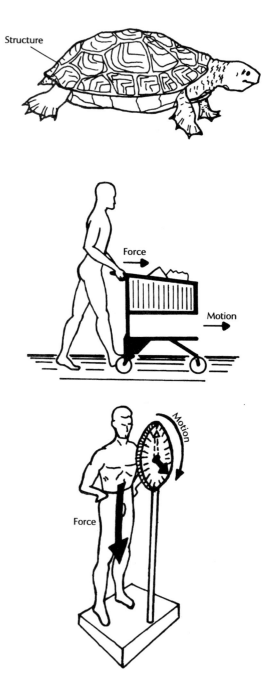

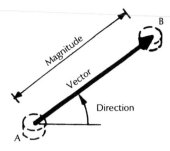

2.1.1.1 A force is a **Vector**. A vector is a parameter (a physical quantity) characterised by a magnitude (or 'intensity') and a direction. Relying on the correlation between force and motion, it is convenient to visualise a vector in terms of motion: when an object moves from point A to point B, the magnitude of the distance travelled is not enough to define the position of point B, relative to A. We need to know the direction as well. Distance, like force, is a vector (see *Displacement* below).

A vector is described graphically as an arrow, pointing in the direction of the vector and having a length representative of the magnitude.

2.1.1.2 Units of measurement

Force, like distance, is one of the fundamental physical entities, measured in one of the basic units. The basic force unit is the Newton (denoted N) and its multiples – kilo-Newton (kN, one thousand Newtons) and Mega-Newton (MN, one million Newtons). As a rule, the international system of units is used throughout this text, with some exceptions. This system employs the Newton (N) and its derivatives for force units, and the metre (m) or millimetre (mm) as length units. Centimetre (cm) is also used occasionally.

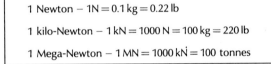

2.1.1.3 *Load*: A force applied to a structure by the environment or by any object (including the structure itself or other structures). Alternative definition: any *External force* applied to the structure, other than a *Reaction force* (definitions of *External force* and *Reaction force* are given in Chapter 3). Other types of forces in structures are encountered in Chapter 3.

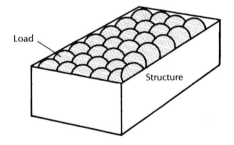

2.1.2 Types of loads on structures

The structures in question are buildings, bridges, monuments, signposts etc. There are two major types of loads: *Gravity loads*, which are usually vertical, and *Environmental loads*, which are often horizontal (e.g. earthquake) but can generally take any direction. Note that although all loads were defined as arising from the influence of the environment, the term *Environmental load* refers to a subclass of loads defined below.

2.1.2.1 *Gravity loads* are the effect of the **weight** of objects on the structure, including the weight of the structure itself (weight is a force). Two kinds are distinguished:

❑ *Dead load*: Load resulting from the self weight (SW) of the structure and of any permanently attached components, such as walls, flooring, permanent partitions etc.
❑ *Live load*: Load arising from the function of the structure, including attached components whose location is not fixed, such as movable partitions.

Live loads are a result of the weight of the loading objects (vehicles, furniture, goods, people etc.) and are mostly vertical (snow load is also considered live load). In some cases, however, loads may be applied in non vertical directions, for instance loads due to braking of vehicles, loads transmitted through pulleys, earth or hydrostatic pressure etc.

2.1.2.2 *Environmental loads* are not a direct result of the weight of objects, but of **movement** in the structure's environment. The most common environmental loads are *Wind load* and *Earthquake load*. Wind load is a result of moving air hitting the structure. Earthquake load is a result of the movement of the earth in which the structure is founded.

The force–movement relation is reciprocal. In the same way that force causes movement, force can be caused by movement. In the above instances, the movement (of the air or the ground) causes forces on the structure and these forces, in turn, cause movement of the structure and of parts of the structure relative to one another.

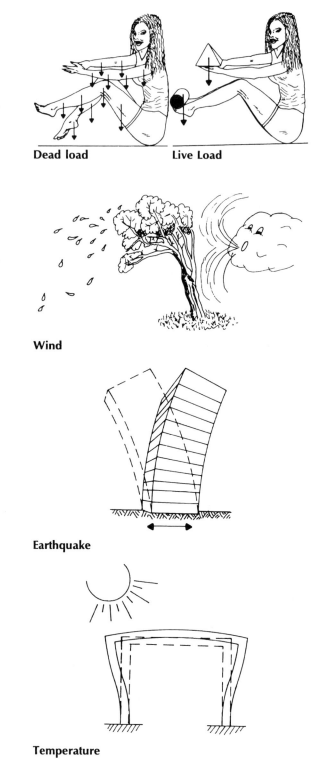

Dead load   **Live Load**

Wind

Earthquake

Temperature

2.1.3 Other environmental influences

Other environmental influences are **movements** which may cause *Internal forces* in certain structures (Chapter 5). In other cases they only cause *Deformations*. These influences include **temperature** effects – change of temperature or temperature difference over parts of the structure, e.g. between the inside and the outside; *Support settlement* – settlement (sinking) of foundations by differing amounts; and so on.

> Some other influences affecting dimensions of components of the structure are also considered environmental effects because of the similarity to the influence of temperature and settlement. These include statistical variation in component dimensions ('lack of fit'), and deliberately induced *Deformations* (*Prestress*, see Chapter 8).

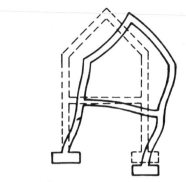

Support settlement

2.1.4 Load distribution

So far, load has been described in general terms, as the overall force acting on the structure, causing movement in it. In practice, a load applied to a structure is **distributed**, or 'spread', over its surface in certain ways, for instance snow over the roof surface, vehicles over a bridge deck etc. A load distributed over a portion of the structure is termed *Distributed load*.

2.1.4.1 Units of measurement
A load distributed over an area is measured in units of force/area:

$$1\,\text{N/m}^2 = \text{Pascal (Pa)}$$

This is a very small load and is rarely used.

$$1000\,\text{N/m}^2 = 1\,\text{kN/m}^2 = \text{kilo-Pascal (kPa)}$$

This is the commonly employed unit for loads.

Two major types of load distribution are most common:

2.1.4.2 Uniformly distributed load
The load is distributed uniformly over the surface, or over a projection of the surface. The load on a

Self weight   Snow load   Wind load

Uniformly distributed loads on a sloping roof

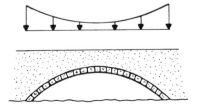

Non uniformly distributed load

unit area of the surface (or its projection) is the same, no matter where this unit area is taken.

2.1.4.3 *Concentrated or Point load*
This is a load distributed over a very small portion of the structure's surface. It is considered as a force acting at a point. Such loads are often exerted by one structural member on another.

2.1.5 *Values of loads for design purpose*
Load values are specified in *Codes* or *Standards*. Codes and standards are design aids, as mentioned in Chapter 1.

2.1.5.1 *Codes* and *Standards*
These are documents produced by authorised national institutes, which prescribe certain requirements to be satisfied by various 'products' including structures.

More specifically, regarding structural design, codes and standards prescribe procedures aimed at ensuring the *Safety* and the *Serviceability* of the structure. Part of these procedures is the specification of the values of loads (and combinations of loads of different types) required to be applied to commonly constructed structures.

> For practical purposes the words 'code' and 'standard' are synonymous. The difference is in their legal status which varies from country to country.

2.1.5.2 *Safety*
The ability of the structure and every part of it to support the load without collapsing, taking into account uncertainties in the values of actual loads and in the strength and behaviour of the structure.

2.1.5.3 *Serviceability*
The ability of the structure to ensure its satisfactory functioning. This implies particularly limitations on the magnitude of movements under various applied loads (*Deflection*, vibration etc.).

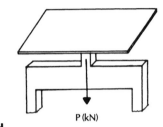

Point load

Characteristic live loads (kN/m^2) (example only)	
Residential buildings:	1.5
Offices (general)	2.0
Public halls (with permanent seating)	4.0
Light industry halls	3.0
Shops: small	3.0
large	5.0
Hotel rooms	2.0
Car parks (no trucks)	3.0

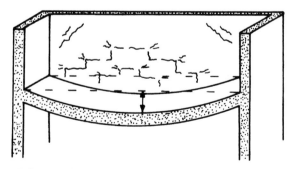

Violation of serviceability

2.2 Movement

Movement is the result of the action of force, or a combination of forces. In general, movement can include such parameters as distance, speed, time, acceleration. In the context of this work only the distance is of interest, both in its own right and as an indicator of the force causing it.

2.2.1 Displacement

Displacement is the **distance** through which a body, or a point on the body, moves as a result of the action of force. This distance is a **vector**. It is characterised by a magnitude – the amount of travel – and a direction.

2.2.2 Rotation

Rotation is a kind of movement (displacement) but it is more complex than the linear movement implied so far. When an object rotates there is a point in it which does not move at all and different points on it have different displacements – different magnitudes and directions of distance.

2.3 Force couple and moment

A rotation cannot be affected by a single force vector of the type we have encountered. Since the body as a whole does not move, there can be no net force acting on it (see force *Resultant* below). We can imagine a rotation of a body if the body is acted upon by two forces of equal magnitude (say P) and opposite direction, such that the lines of action of the two forces are offset by a certain distance (a, say). Such a pair of forces is termed a *Force couple*, or *Couple* for short.

The body as a whole cannot move, because the two forces act in opposite directions. But at each of the two points of application of forces, the corresponding force moves the point in its direction.

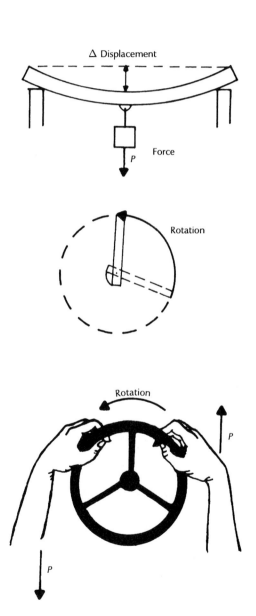

Displacement

Δ Displacement

Force

P

Rotation

Rotation

P

P

The result is that the two points move in opposite directions, causing the rotation of the body.

2.3.1 *Moment*

The effect of a force couple is clearly dependent, not only on the magnitude of the two forces, but also on the distance by which they are offset – the **Lever arm**. If the arm was zero – the forces were collinear – there would be no rotation The effect of lever arm length on such activities as bolt tightening or releasing is well known.

In order to express the effect of the force couple which takes into account both force magnitude and lever arm a parameter termed **Moment** is defined (denoted M), whose magnitude is the product of the force magnitude and the lever arm length: $M = P \times a$. It is customary to display a moment graphically as a curved arrow showing the **sense** of rotation, instead of showing the system of force couple. This arrow does not represent a vector – it has only a sense, not a magnitude and not a specific direction.

Units of measurement of moment are force × length, such as Newton-millimetre (Nmm), kilo-Newton-metre (kNm) etc.

The force couple defines a plane (two parallel lines). It is intuitively clear that the rotation is not affected by the direction of the forces in this plane, but only by the relative sense of the forces forming the couple, which determines the sense of rotation – clockwise or counterclockwise.

Nevertheless, a moment is, in fact, a vector whose magnitude is defined above and whose direction is **perpendicular** to the plane of the force couple, and with a sense related to the sense of rotation in a 'right handed' manner. Any operation on vectors, as detailed in subsequent sections, is applicable also to moments, but due to the difficulty in three-dimensional visualisation, this topic is not pursued further. Furthermore, the vectorial nature of moment is not essential for the understanding of structural behaviour at the fundamental level.

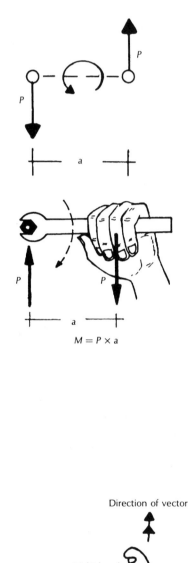

$$M = P \times a$$

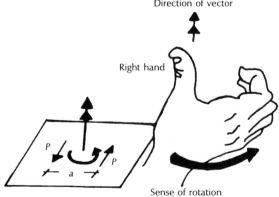

Direction of vector

Right hand

Sense of rotation

2.4 Resultant force

Normally a structure is not subjected to a single force, but to a combination of several loads and other forces, in different directions and locations. In order to understand how the structure responds to such load combinations, it is necessary to know how to handle such combinations – how to operate with vectors.

2.4.1 Summation of vectors – resultant

When a number of forces (or any vectors) act on an object simultaneously, the **Resultant force** (or **Resultant vector**) is a single force (vector) which, if acting alone on the object would have the same effect as the combined forces (vectors). It is said to represent the sum of the vectors, or the **Vectorial sum**.

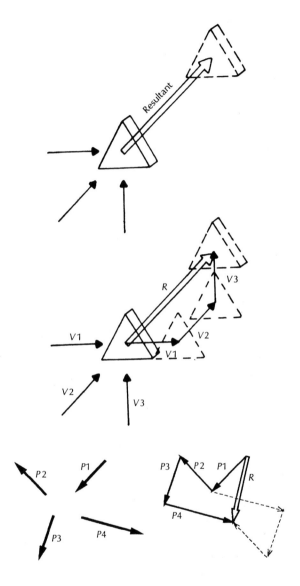

2.4.1.1 It is easy to visualise a resultant vector and a way to derive it if we think of displacements rather than forces. If we think of each vector as a corresponding displacement, and instead of applying them simultaneously apply them sequentially (the final result being the same), then the resultant displacement is the distance from the starting point to the final point.

To obtain the resultant graphically, plot the individual vectors tail to head. The resultant is the vector joining the tail of the first vector with the head of the last.

Satisfy yourself that the order of plotting the vectors does not affect the resultant, by trying different plotting sequences.

2.5 Coordinate systems

The description of vectors and operations with vectors given above relies on graphic and visual tools. In order to provide quantitative computational procedures, a system of reference, termed

Coordinate system, is defined. Coordinate systems are analytical constructs designed to give a quantifiable description of space.

2.5.1 Coordinates in the plane

In order to define the position of a point A in the plane, relative to a fixed point – the **Origin** of the system (o) – two **Coordinates** are needed. For example, the distance of the point from the origin and the angle this distance forms with a fixed direction – an **Axis** – uniquely defines the position of the point. Alternatively the position can be provided by two distances measured perpendicularly to two axes.

2.5.2 Coordinates in space

In a similar manner, to define the position of a point in space, relative to the origin, three coordinates are required – a distance (from the origin) and two angles (with respect to two axes), two distances and an angle, or three distances.

The number of coordinates required to define the position of a point (relative to the origin) is termed the **Dimensionality** of the system – the plane is two dimensional whereas space is three dimensional.

2.5.3 Cartesian coordinates

The coordinate system which is most widely employed is the **Cartesian coordinate system**. In this system, the position of a point is given by its distances from two orthogonal (mutually perpendicular) axes in plane, or to three axes in space. (Named after René Descartes, French mathematician, 1596–1650.)

2.6 Vector components

In general, a vector is given by a length (the magnitude) and a direction. The length of a line connecting two points A and B, in a Cartesian coordinate

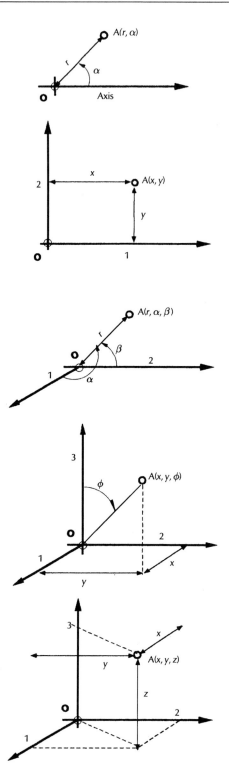

system, is given by the square root of the sum of squares of the differences in the coordinates of the two points (by Pythagoras' theorem):

In plane: $\ell = \sqrt{\Delta x^2 + \Delta y^2}$

In space: $\ell = \sqrt{\Delta x^2 + \Delta y^2 + \Delta z^2}$

A vector **V** can be considered as the distance between two points, A and B – the 'tail' point A (the start) and the 'head' point B (the end). The length of the vector is given by the expression above. The 'direction' or 'sense' of the vector – from A to B, or from B to A – is determined by the algebraic **signs** of the coordinate differences. The coordinates of the 'from' point (the tail) are subtracted from those of the 'to' point (the head):

From A to B:

$\Delta x = x_B - x_A; \quad \Delta y = y_B - y_A; \quad (\Delta z = z_B - z_A)$

From B to A:

$\Delta x = x_A - x_B; \quad \Delta y = y_A - y_B; \quad (\Delta z = z_A - z_B)$

The coordinate differences between the vector's end points are termed the **Components** of the vector. A vector (**V**) is fully described by two components in plane (V_x, V_y), and three components in space (V_x, V_y, V_z). The subscripts indicate the direction (axis) of the component. **Components are Scalars** – they have only magnitude and sign. Thus the use of coordinate systems enables dealing with vectors by means of their scalar components, which are subject to normal algebraic operations.

2.7 Vector summation in the Cartesian system

Summing of vectors now reduces to summing their components, as is clearly demonstrated by performing the graphic summation in the framework of the coordinate system:

$$R_x = V1_x + V2_x + \cdots = \sum (V_x);$$

$$R_y = \sum (V_y)$$

$$= V1_y + V2_y + \cdots$$

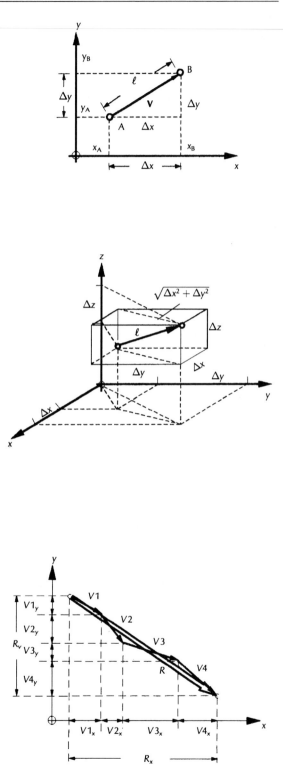

where R_x, R_y are components of the resultant force and $\sum(\cdots)=$ the sum of terms in the parentheses.

2.8 Summation of moments

In the plane, moments can be treated as scalars, since the direction of the force couples forming them is not significant (the resultant force is zero in any case), but only the sense of rotation. Defining a positive sense as, say, counterclockwise turns a moment into a signed scalar, enabling the arithmetic summation of moments.

> In the general case, summation of moments can be performed as summation of vectors using the definition of moment vectors given above. In the quite rare case of having to sum moments in space, this can still be done without reference to the vectorial nature of the moment. One way of doing this is to project the forces forming each couple onto the principal planes (the x–y, x–z, and y–z planes), and then summing moments in each plane separately.

2.9 Resultant force location

2.9.1 Parallel forces

The magnitude of the resultant of a set of parallel forces is simply the sum of the forces and the direction is parallel with the forces. The question is the **location** of the resultant relative to a reference point.

To obtain the location of the resultant force, apply at the reference point imaginary forces of equal magnitude and opposite sense to the given forces. These imaginary forces form couples with the original forces. Their sum forms a couple with the resultant force.

The location of the resultant force is determined from the condition that its moment is equal to the sum of the moments of the given forces. This is

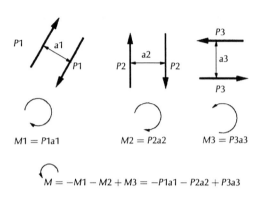

$M1 = P1a1 \qquad M2 = P2a2 \qquad M3 = P3a3$

$M = -M1 - M2 + M3 = -P1a1 - P2a2 + P3a3$

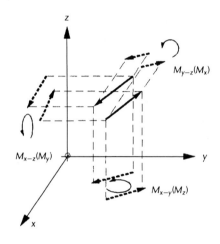

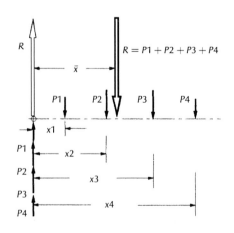

$R = P1 + P2 + P3 + P4$

because the effect of the resultant has to be the same as that of the given forces in every respect, including rotation with respect to any point. Thus:

$$M_R = R \times \bar{x} = P1 \times x1 + P2 \times x2 + \cdots$$

$$= \sum (P \times x)$$

$$\bar{x} = \frac{P1x1 + P2x2 + \cdots}{P1 + P2 + \cdots} = \frac{\sum (P \times x)}{\sum (P)}$$

2.9.2 *General system of forces*

This expression can be used to obtain the **location** of the origin (the application point) of the resultant of any set of forces (not necessarily parallel), by working with their components. Each force is replaced by its components, having the same point of application as the force.

The components parallel to any axis (x, y) form a set of parallel forces and so the expression above gives the location of the **component** of the resultant parallel to the same axis (i.e. its distance from the axis). The origin of the resultant is at the intersection of the directions of the two components.

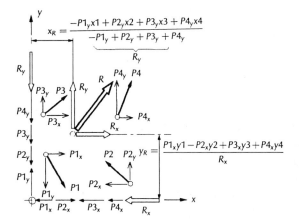

3 Forces in Structures – Equilibrium

3.1 Equilibrium

When a body is subjected to the action of several forces, the combination of forces can be such that the body **does not move** – the forces 'cancel' one another's effect. The simplest example is two forces of equal magnitude and opposite senses acting on the body along the same line. When such a situation exists, the body or the forces are said to be in *Equilibrium* (a Latin word meaning 'equal weight' as on the two arms of a scale).

The study of forces in equilibrium is termed *Statics*, indicating the absence of motion.

3.1.1 Conditions for equilibrium

The condition of no movement implies that to maintain equilibrium, the resultants of all forces and of all couples must vanish. Since couples and forces are different entities, having different units, the resultants must be considered separately.

In graphical terms, the first condition (vanishing of the force resultant) implies that, in a state of equilibrium, **forces, when drawn tail to head, form a closed polygon**, i.e., the head of the last force vector touches the tail of the first. This can be a useful tool for force analysis in certain simple cases – see truss example in 4.8.

The rule applies also to moments, when considered as vectors. However in the plane it is more convenient to treat moments as signed scalars and sum them algebraically.

In Cartesian coordinates, the requirement for equilibrium reduces to simple algebraic expression:

x direction:

$$P1_x + P2_x + \cdots = 0 \Rightarrow \sum (P_x) = 0$$

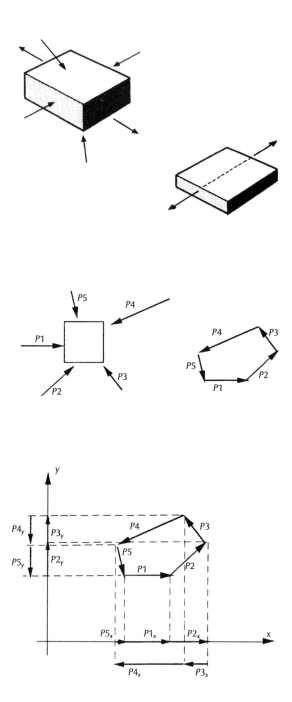

y direction:

$$P1_y + P2_y + \cdots = 0 \Rightarrow \sum (P_y) = 0$$

(in three dimensions, *z* direction: $\sum (P_z) = 0$)

Moments: $M1 + M2 + \cdots = 0 \Rightarrow \sum (M) = 0$

The expression states that the sum of force components in the direction of each of the axes, and the sum of all moments, vanish.

3.1.2 *Equilibrium and structures*

In most cases, architectural structures, or any part of a structure, do not move once loads have been applied (dynamic situations such as during earthquake or vibration are not considered here). **An architectural structure and every part of it is in equilibrium**. This simple and apparently obvious statement is the principal tool enabling the analysis of the behaviour of structures and of the forces acting on and in them.

3.1.3 *Overall equilibrium of a structure*

The loads applied to a structure are, in general, not in equilibrium. Furthermore, some of the loads are changing and variable, and yet the structure is (usually) stationary, i.e. in equilibrium. In order to ensure this state of affairs, it is clear that other forces act on the structure, which are **always** in equilibrium with the applied loads. These forces are termed *Reactions* – they 'react' to the loads to keep the structure in equilibrium. The reactions are provided by the structure's *Supports* – usually the foundations, or by another structure, considered separately.

A force **causing** motion can be considered an **acting** force. A force **restraining** motion can likewise be considered as **reacting**.

3.2 Displacement components

The role of the supports is to prevent movement of the structure as a whole (as a 'rigid body'), i.e.

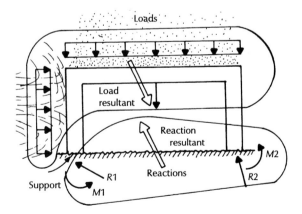
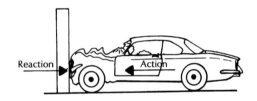

to **prevent displacements and rotations** at the points of support.

Since displacements are vectors they can be considered through their **components**. Any point in the plane has therefore two **possible** displacement components and one possible rotation, or, in all, three *Degrees of freedom* – possible components of displacement and rotation. Due to the correspondence between displacements and forces the term 'degree of freedom' refers also to possible force components.

A degree of freedom is a theoretical concept. A general object in the plane has three degrees of freedom – three **potential** directions of motion. Some of these may be **free** (to move), while others may be **restrained**.

To avoid confusion, the word displacement is assigned to what is more rigorously termed *Translation*, and rotations are treated separately. Strictly, rotation is a type of displacement, as commented above. A point in space has six degrees of freedom – three translation components and three rotation components (or planes of rotation).

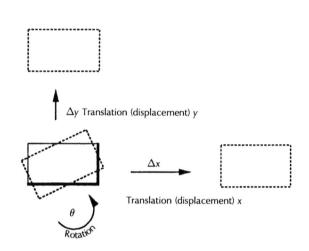

Degrees of freedom in the plane

3.3 Supports

3.3.1 Relation between displacements and reactions

To maintain the structure in equilibrium, it is often not necessary to restrain **all** degrees of freedom at the supports. In general, to prevent the movement of a structure, or any body in the plane, it is sufficient to restrain three degrees of freedom. If the structure (body) has more than one support, not all three degrees of freedom need to be restrained in each support.

To restrain a displacement, a force has to be applied in the direction of that displacement, in the opposite sense. To restrain rotation a couple (a moment) has to be applied in the opposite sense. These forces or moments are *Reaction components*. In all, there may be up to three reaction components in a support in the plane (two forces and one moment). In space there may be up to six reaction components at a support – three forces and three moments (in three planes).

There is a reciprocal relation between reaction forces and the corresponding displacements. As we have seen, a force (or moment) causes displacement (or rotation) in its direction. With regard to reaction components, however:

In directions where the support allows displacement (or rotation) there is no reaction, and vice versa, in a direction where displacement (or rotation) is restrained, there is a reaction.

By definition, reactions are forces whose function it is to restrain movement, which would be otherwise caused by the applied loads.

3.3.2 Types of supports

As mentioned above, when the structure has more than one support, not all degrees of freedom need to be restrained at every support, and it is often advantageous to restrain only some of the degrees of freedom at a support. For instance it can make the support (e.g. the foundation) simpler and cheaper if it does not need to restrain rotation.

Supports are characterised by the degrees of freedom which they restrain. There are three main types of supports in the plane. These types are listed below in descending order of restraint.

It is important to note that this classification of supports is an idealisation for analysis purposes. A support rarely completely restrains, nor completely releases motion. The idealisation is valid only to the extent that analytical results do not deviate from actual behaviour significantly.

There are conventional graphic symbols used to indicate the type of support, for analytical purposes. These symbols do not resemble the actual appearance of the support (see also *line diagrams* and *joints* – 3.6 below). These symbols accompany the list of planar support types given below.

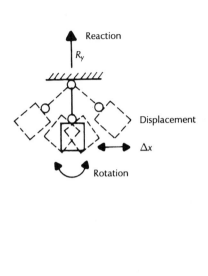

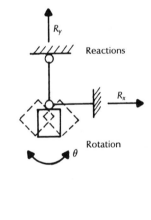

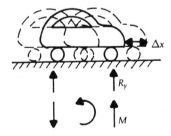

Relations between free and restrained degrees of freedom

3.3.2.1 *Fixed support*

All degrees of freedom are restrained. There are three reaction components – two force components and a moment.

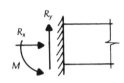
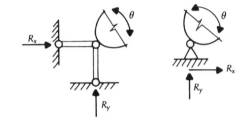

Fixed support

3.3.2.2 *Hinged (pinned) support*

The two displacement components are restrained, the rotation is free. There are two reaction components – forces. There is no moment. This is the simplest support to achieve in practice (especially as foundation), and is often termed a *Simple support*.

Hinged (pinned) support

3.3.2.3 *Roller support*

Roller support or simply 'roller' restrains one direction of displacement. It allows rotation and displacement perpendicular to the restrained direction. It is often used in bridges (to allow thermal expansion). In buildings it is sometimes introduced in the form of a column hinged at both ends. Because the bottom of the column is free to rotate, the top is free to move sideways (as well as rotate).

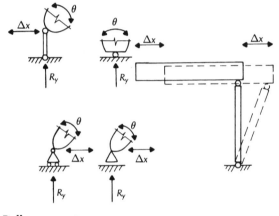

Roller support

3.3.3 *Combination of supports*

Depending on the number of supports in a structure, combinations of supports of different types are possible. If there is only one support, it must obviously be fixed. In other cases the combination must be such that at least three degrees of freedom of the structure are restrained (see also conditions for *stability*, Chapter 7).

More than three degrees of freedom may be restrained (in the plane). In such cases there may be more reaction components than are needed to maintain equilibrium (See *static indeterminacy*, Chapter 5).

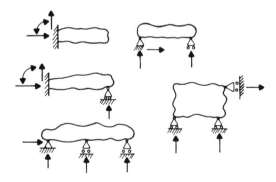

Some combinations of support types

3.4 Internal forces

The forces encountered up to now – loads and reactions – can be considered *External forces*, as they act on the boundary of the structure (or the part of the structure under consideration).

It is intuitively clear that for the reactions to be in equilibrium with the loads, the loads must somehow 'pass' or 'travel' through the structure to the supports, or .put somewhat differently, the structure must 'transfer' the loads to the supports. In fact, this **Load transfer** is the main function of the structure (see 2.1). Understanding the **manner** in which loads are transferred is the essence of understanding structural behaviour.

The somewhat nebulous concept of 'load transfer' implies the presence of *Internal forces* within the structure. Naturally we cannot see them by looking at the whole structure, but if we perform an **imaginary** cut through the structure at any point, it is clear that for the structure not to fall apart every **part** of it has to exert force on every adjacent part.

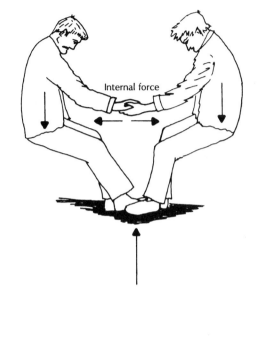

3.4.1 Free-body diagrams

In order to 'see' internal forces in a certain location within the structure, we have to 'cut' the structure at this point. If we now 'cut' the structure at another location we obtain a *Free-body diagram*. By considering the equilibrium of this free body we may be able to compute or evaluate the internal forces in the desired location, provided the free body is judiciously selected.

For instance, if we know the reaction components at a support, we may choose a free body between this support and the location where we want to evaluate the internal forces, and, provided there are not more than two internal force components and an internal moment, we could use the equations of 3.1.1 to compute them.

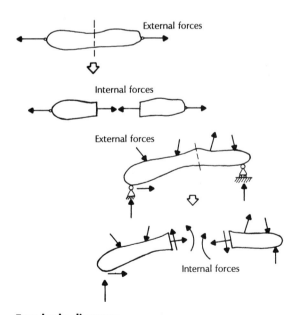

Free-body diagrams

Free-body diagrams are one of the most powerful tools of structural analysis.

Detailed examples of the use of free-body diagrams to compute internal forces are given in Chapter 4.

3.4.2 Deformations

Deformation is a displacement or rotation of a **segment** of the structure corresponding to an internal force and moment, similar to the way in which a displacement (of a point in the structure) corresponds to an external load.

Deformations are in fact the **relative** displacements and rotations between two sections bounding a free-body diagram. As the name implies, deformations measure the extent of **change of shape** – stretching, skewing, bending or twisting – of the structures or of parts of the structure.

Displacement is a movement due to external force, **deformation** is movement due to internal force.

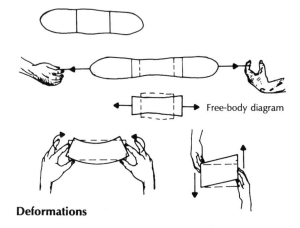

Free-body diagram

Deformations

3.5 Planar and spatial structures

Before proceeding to discuss types of internal forces and deformations it is necessary to characterise certain types of structures.

All structures are three dimensional. This is a fact that engineers and architects seem sometimes to overlook (probably because the representation is usually two dimensional). The terms *Planar structure* or *Plane structure* and *Spatial structure* or *Space structure* refer to the usual mode of analysing the forces in the structure, not to its geometry.

3.5.1 Structural analysis

Structural analysis consists of resolving the internal forces in a structure, and the displacements at selected points. It is possible to analyse a planar

Planar structure

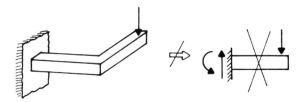

Spatial structure

structure by looking at forces (and displacements) in separate planes, because forces in one plane do not significantly affect forces in another. In spatial structures this is not possible and it is necessary to look at a three-dimensional representation (e.g. free-body diagram) and resolve forces in three-dimensional coordinate systems.

While the principles of analysis are similar in the two cases, the application and visualisation are considerably more complex in spatial structures. For this reason, most of the discussion and examples of analytical principles are referred to planar structures in this and following chapters. Examples of spatial structures and characterisation of the internal forces in them are presented in Part II.

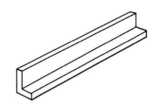

Bar

3.6 Bar structures

A *Bar* or a *Member* is a structure or part of a structure in which one dimension (the length) exceeds the other two dimensions several times (say at least three-fold). A *Bar structure*, or the equivalent terms *Member structure*, *Reticulated structure*, *Lattice structure*, is a structure consisting of several bars joined together.

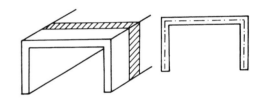

Planar bar structure

3.6.1 Planar bar structures

The vast majority of planar structures are, or can be considered, bar structures. Even a structure consisting of planar (or cylindrical) surfaces can often be 'sliced' into identical narrow strips, each consisting of bars. Such a structure is a planar bar structure, in the analytical sense, despite its three-dimensional geometry (See *Slab*, Chapter 8 and *Barrel vault*, Chapter 9).

3.6.1.1 Graphic representation
Because of the proportion of the length relative to the width of a bar, a bar is often drawn as a line, and the structure as a whole as a network of lines

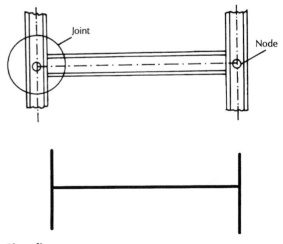

Line diagram

through the centres of bars – a *Line diagram* of the structure. These lines are not necessarily straight, although they often are.

3.6.2 Nodes, joints and connections

A *Node* is the theoretical point at which the centrelines of joining bars intersect. This term is used in the context of line diagrams. Nodes may be defined, for analytical purposes, also at intermediate points along members.

The term *Joint* is used more freely to denote either 'node' or the physical properties of the intersection of members (see below). Supports (3.3) are joints at the boundaries of the structure.

Connection denotes the physical dimension and detail of the joining of bars (members).

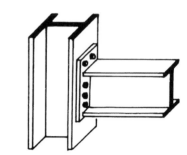

Connection

3.6.2.1 Types of joints

As in the case of supports, joints are idealised for the purpose of force analysis of the structure. The actual appearance and behaviour of the joint are usually quite different from the graphic and analytical representation. The idealisation is valid only so long as the actual behaviour does not differ significantly from the idealised. Two major types of joints are distinguished:

- ❑ *Rigid joint*: A joint in which the angle between members is unchanged – relative rotation of the members is restrained (though rotation of the joint as a whole is not).
- ❑ *Hinged joint*, *Pin joint*, sometimes termed *Simple joint* allows free rotation of the joining members relative to one another, and therefore change of the angle between them.

There are joints defined as *Semi-rigid joints*, which allow some, but not free, rotation between the joining members. This type, although used in practice, is not well defined from the analytical viewpoint and is rarely used in analysis.

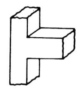
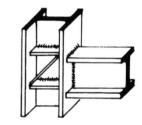

Rigid joint

Line diagram

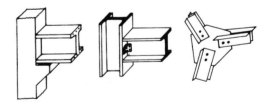

Pin joints

Line diagram

3.6.3 Cross-section

In member structures the fictitious 'cut' performed to obtain free-body diagrams, in order to view internal forces, is performed as a plane cut perpendicular to the axis of the member. Unless specifically mentioned otherwise, the term *Cross-section* when used in the context of member structures is understood to be such a 'cut'. The term may also refer to the **shape** of the planar area obtained by such a section (e.g. 'rectangular cross-section', 'circular cross-section', etc.).

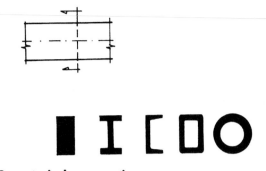

Some typical cross-sections

3.7 Internal force components

In general, there must be a correspondence between the number of internal forces (including internal moments) and the number of degrees of freedom in a point (node) in the member (3.2), because each degree of freedom corresponds to a possible displacement (or rotation) and therefore there must be a force corresponding to that degree of freedom which causes the displacement.

It follows that three internal force components are defined for planar structures – two forces and one moment. In bar structures these forces are related to the axis of the member. To 'see' these forces we cut short free-body diagrams by parallel sections, perpendicular to the axis of the member. The forces and their corresponding deformations are defined below.

3.7.1 Axial force

Axial force is a force along the axis of the member (perpendicular to the cross-section). Two types are distinguished, according to the deformations they cause: *Tension* causes *Elongation* of the member. *Compression* causes *Shortening* of the member. It is conventional in computation to consider tension as a positive axial force and compression as negative.

Tension and compression are the basic internal forces in the theory of structures. It is possible

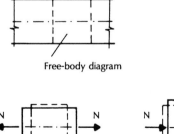

Free-body diagram

Tension   Compression

Axial force

(though not always convenient) to understand structural behaviour without recourse to any other type of force.

3.7.2 Shear force

Shear force is a force acting perpendicular to the member's axis, i.e. parallel to the cross-section. For equilibrium, the shear forces on the two cross-sections of the free-body diagram must act in opposite senses, causing a **Shear deformation** which 'skews' it – turns it from a rectangle into a parallelogram.

A state of pure shear in members is rare, because the shear forces on a free-body diagram form a couple. To maintain equilibrium, a bending moment of opposing sense is normally present.

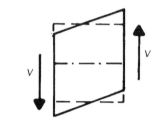

Shear force

3.7.3 Bending moment

Bending moment is a force **couple** on each of the cross-sections bounding the free-body diagram (usually in opposing senses, for equilibrium). The resulting **Bending** or **Flexure** deformation is a rotation of the two cross-sections, relative to each other, turning the rectangular free-body diagram into a trapezoid (wedge shape). This deformation causes elongation on one side of the member and shortening on the opposing side. For this to happen the elongating side must become convex and the shortening side concave.

It can clearly be seen that, in fact, tension is caused near one side and compression at the other, thus demonstrating the primacy of these types of forces. Note that **the convex side is in tension and the concave side in compression**. This is a helpful tool in the analysis of bending.

At the end of a member connected to a hinged joint or support there can be no bending moment, because the hinge allows free rotation and cannot resist a moment. An exception is when an external couple is actually applied at the member's end, but this is a rare occurrence.

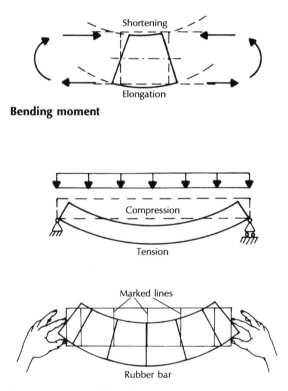

Bending moment

Demonstration of bending

3.7.4 Action

The term *Action* or *Action mode*, when referring to structural analysis and behaviour, means the state of internal forces to which the structure or member is subjected. We talk of axial action when the bar is in tension or compression, of bending action or flexure, when it is subject to bending moment (usually accompanied by shear as well). Naturally, a bar can be subject to a combination of 'actions' such as compression and bending, etc.

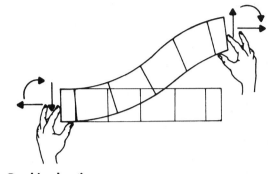

Combined action

4 Computational Examples

4.1 Principles

As mentioned in Chapter 3 (3.4) it is often possible to evaluate internal forces in a desired cross-section in the structure, by considering a free-body diagram bounded by this cross-section and another cross-section, or a support, where the forces (or reactions) are known. Internal forces are the major design parameters, since their magnitude determines the size of the structural members (see Chapter 6).

The internal forces, and the way they vary over the structure, depend primarily on the shape of the structure. In order to appreciate the relation between form and forces in the structure, it is therefore important to be able to estimate the magnitude of internal forces, at least in a qualitative manner. The purpose of this chapter is to demonstrate the procedure for estimating internal forces, using some simple, basic structures as illustrations.

4.2 Example 1: simply supported beam

Beam
A bar acting in bending and shear (3.7.2, 3.7.3).

Simply supported beam
A beam supported at one end on a hinged support and at the other on a roller (3.3.3).

> The roller is a computational device to ensure there are no more than three reaction components (if both supports were hinged there would be four reaction components). In practice both supports are often hinged, except where freedom of movement is important, e.g. to avoid thermal stresses – bridges are a typical example.

A simply supported beam is one of the most widespread structures. It also serves as a basis for

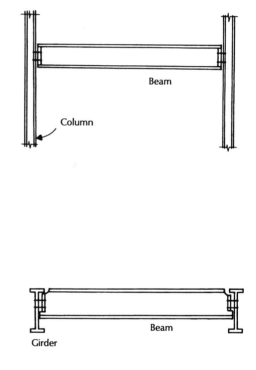

Simply supported beam

understanding many other types of structures, typically structures spanning between two supports or sets of supports.

Span
The distance between the supports of the beam.

4.2.1 Data

Given: A simply supported beam with span L (m), loaded by a uniformly distributed load q (units – kN/m).

Distributed load on a bar has dimension of force/length. For instance, the beam may be supporting a floor of width b (m), or the beam is part of a system of beams spaced b (m) apart and supporting the floor (Chapter 8). If the floor is uniformly loaded by a load of w (kN/m²), then the load on the beam is obtained by multiplying w by the width b: $q = b \times w$ (kN/m).

Required: (a) The internal forces at the centre of the span; (b) the internal forces at an arbitrary cross-section at a distance x from the left support (A).

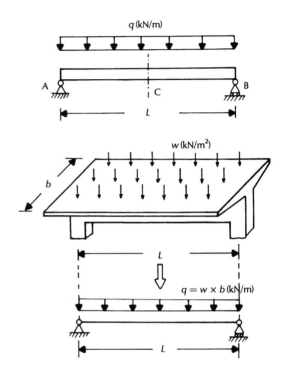

4.2.2 Forces at mid span

Step 1: *computation of reactions*

In accordance with section 3.3 the beam has three reaction components: two forces at the hinged support and one at the roller. According to 3.1, there are three equilibrium equations: (1) vanishing of the sums of forces in the x (horizontal) direction; (2) vanishing of the sums of forces in the y (vertical) direction; (3) vanishing of the sum of moments (couples). There are, then, enough equations to compute the three unknown reactions.

4.2.2.1 First, the resultant of the applied load needs to be computed. The resultant of a load uniformly distributed along a length L is the load

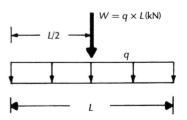

multiplied by the length. If the load per 1 m is q kN, then the load over L m is $q \times L$ kN. The resultant $W = q \times L$ acts at the centre of the span (by symmetry).

For a general (non uniformly) distributed load, varying as a function of the distance x, the resultant is the area under the load function over the given length, and it is located in the centroid of this area. For instance, the resultant of triangularly distributed load with q_0 (kN/m) at one end and zero at the other is $q_0 L/2$, and it is located $\frac{1}{3}L$ from the end with q_0.

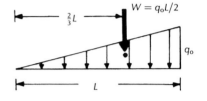

This result can be obtained from 2.9 – resultant of parallel forces, by assuming the load over small segments to be uniformly distributed (replacing the smooth line with a stepped line). The value of the uniformly distributed load in each segment is the average value of the load – the load at mid segment. Compute the resultant load for each segment and then the resultant is the sum of these segmental forces and its location is determined by 2.9. As the segments are made smaller, the sum of segmental forces approaches the area of the load function and its location, the centroid of this area (see also 5.5.2.3).

4.2.2.2 Equilibrium equations
Sum of horizontal forces:

$$\sum (P_x) = 0 \Rightarrow H_A = 0$$

Since H_A is the only possible horizontal force, it must vanish to maintain equilibrium in the horizontal direction.

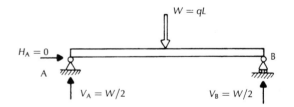

Sum of vertical forces:

$$\sum (P_y) = 0 \Rightarrow V_A + V_B - W = 0$$
$$\Rightarrow V_A + V_B = W$$

'Up' is considered 'positive' in the equation. From symmetry conditions it can be deduced that:

$$V_A = V_B = W/2$$

4.2.2.3 In general (when the load is not symmetric) we would need to use the third equation (sum of moments):

$$\sum (M) = 0$$

This equation is highly significant as it represents the equilibrium between the moment of the external load trying to 'overturn' the structure and the moment of the internal forces or the reaction forces which stabilise it.

To demonstrate this interpretation of equilibrium, let us compute the reaction V_B by looking at a free-body diagram between support A and 'just' in front of support B. The overturning couple consists of the forces W with lever arm $L/2$, trying to turn the beam clockwise round A. The stabilising couple consists of forces V_B and lever arm L, restraining this rotation. Taking counterclockwise as 'positive' the equation yields:

$$V_B \times L - W \times L/2 = 0 \Rightarrow V_B = W/2$$

V_A can then be obtained from the force equilibrium in the vertical direction ($V_A = W - V_B = W/2$), or from a similar moment equation for rotation round B.

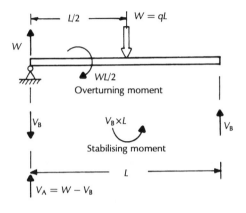

Step 2: *computation of internal forces at C*

4.2.2.4 As mentioned above, to compute the internal forces at C (centre of the span), we need to look at a free-body diagram bounded by C and a point where the forces are known, in this case support A or support B (it makes no difference which). In order to consider equilibrium, we have to show **all** the forces acting on the free-body diagram, including loads, reactions and the (unknown) internal forces.

In the case of a bar of a planar structure, there can be up to three internal force components – Axial force, N, shear force, V, and a bending moment, M (3.7). We have to assume that all three forces exist. The direction of each force can be arbitrarily assumed. If the sign of any force (or moment) is computed as negative, its actual sense is opposed to the one assumed.

There are three unknown forces – the internal forces – and three equilibrium equations, so it should be possible to compute the internal forces.

4.2.2.5 As in the case of the reactions, we first compute the resultant of the applied loads on the free-body diagram. The resultant is $W/2 = qL/2$, and it acts at the centre of the half-beam, i.e. at a distance of $L/4$ from the support.

Computation of the axial and shear forces from force equilibrium is straightforward:

$$\sum (P_x) = 0 \Rightarrow N_C = 0;$$

$$\sum (P_y) = 0 \Rightarrow V_C + W/2 - W/2 = 0 \Rightarrow V_C = 0$$

4.2.2.6 In order to compute the bending moment, we consider the free-body diagram as subjected to two couples: the 'overturning' couple with load $W/2$ and lever arm $L/4$, and the 'stabilising' couple -- the internal couple (the bending moment). The moment equilibrium then yields (considering counterclockwise positive):

$$\sum (M) = 0 \Rightarrow M_C - (W/2)(L/4) = 0$$

$$\Rightarrow M_C = WL/8 = qL^2/8$$

4.2.2.7 The positive result for M_C indicates that its sense is counterclockwise as initially assumed, meaning that there is compression in the top 'fibre' of the beam and tension at the bottom (3.7.3). This result is intuitively correct if we consider the way the beam bends, with the top being concave (and hence shortening), and the bottom convex (and hence elongating).

4.2.2.8 The result $M_C = qL^2/8$ is well known and important, as it recurs in many contexts, and serves as a basis for many computations in structural analysis. From symmetry and simple

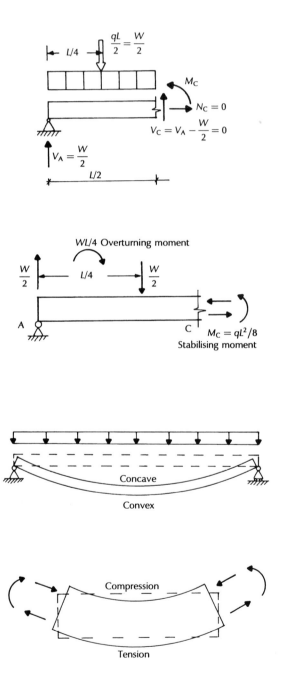

reasoning, it is apparent that this is the maximum value of the bending moment, which decreases towards the supports, where it vanishes, by definition of the simple supports (3.3).

4.2.3 General solution

4.2.3.1 The first step, computation of reactions, is identical with (4.2.2) (same beam – same reactions).

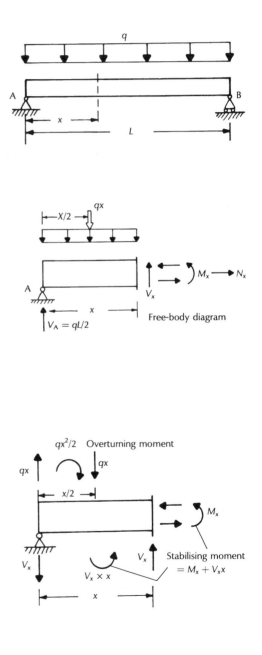

4.2.3.2 The second step is similar to that of (4.2.2), except that instead of taking a free-body diagram of length $L/2$, we take a free-body diagram of arbitrary length x from support A.

4.2.3.3 The load resultant is qx and it is located at $x/2$ from support A. The force equilibrium equations yield:

$$\sum (P_x) = 0 \Rightarrow N_x = 0$$
$$\sum (P_y) = 0 \Rightarrow V_x + qL/2 - qx = 0$$
$$\Rightarrow V_x = qx - qL/2 = q(x - L/2)$$

Free-body diagram

The shear force is 'negative', i.e. directed 'downwards' on the free-body diagram when the section is to the left of mid span $(x < L/2)$ and upwards to the right of mid span.

4.2.3.4 Computation of the bending moment based on moment equilibrium is similar, in principle, to (4.2.2), but somewhat more involved. Due to the non-vanishing of the shear force, the stabilising moment is produced by two couples: the bending moment, and the shear force with lever arm of x:

$$\sum (M) = 0 \Rightarrow M_x + V_x \times x - (qx)(x/2) = 0$$
$$\Rightarrow M_x = qx^2/2 - V_x \times x$$

Substituting the value of V_x computed above yields:

$$M_x = (qx^2/2) - x(qx - qL/2)$$
$$= qx^2/2 - qx^2 + qLx/2$$
$$\underline{M_x = -qx^2/2 + qLx/2 = qx/2(L - x)}$$

4.2.3.5 Note that M is positive for any value of x between zero and L, meaning that the top fibre is compressed and the bottom fibre tensioned, along the whole beam.

4.2.3.6 The above computations demonstrate the general procedure for computing internal forces in a member of any structure: Draw a free-body diagram from a point where the forces are known, to an **arbitrarily selected** cross-section and compute the internal forces at that cross-section based on equilibrium equations. The result yields the **variation** of the forces along the member selected.

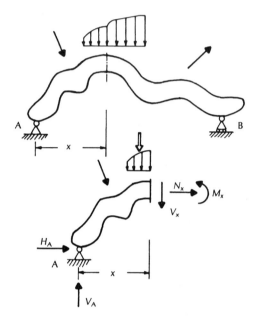

4.3 Example 2: cantilever beam

Cantilever beam (or, simply, **cantilever**)
A beam supported at one end by a fixed support (3.2.1) – the 'fixed end'. The other end is free (no support at all).

4.3.1 Data

Given: A cantilever beam of length L, loaded by a uniformly distributed load q.

Required: The internal forces at any cross-section and the reactions at the fixed end.

4.3.2 General solution

4.3.2.1 This case is computationally simpler than the simply supported beam. There is no need to compute reactions first (although it is possible to do so, in a manner similar to the simply supported beam). We can always select a free-body diagram from the free end to the cross-section at which forces are required, since the forces at the free end

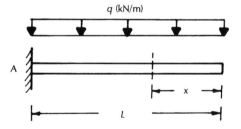

are known in advance – they all vanish, as there are no reactions. We shall call the distance of an arbitrary cross-section from the free end, x.

4.3.2.2 The resultant of the applied load is: $qx/2$, and it is located at the mid point of the free-body diagram, i.e. a distance $x/2$ from the free end.

Force equilibrium equations yield the following results for the internal axial and shear forces:

$$\sum (P_x) = 0 \Rightarrow N_x = 0$$

$$\sum (P_y) = 0 \Rightarrow V_x - q \times x = 0 \Rightarrow V_x = q \times x$$

4.3.2.3 It is apparent that the beam bends such that its upper side is convex, and therefore in tension, so it is natural to assume the internal couple in a sense which produces tension in the upper fibre and compression in the lower. The shear force produces, with the applied load resultant, a couple with force qx and lever arm $x/2$ – the 'overturning' moment. The stabilising moment is produced by the internal couple (bending moment) M_x. The moment equilibrium equation yields the value of the bending moment:

$$\sum M = 0 \Rightarrow M_x - q \times x(x/2) = 0$$

$$\Rightarrow \underline{M_x = qx^2/2}$$

4.3.3 Reactions – fixed-end forces

To obtain the reactions, we simply need to substitute $x = L$ in the expressions for the internal forces, since at the support the reactions are the internal forces. The result:

$$H_A = 0; \quad V_A = qL; \quad M_A = qL^2/2$$

The values of the reactions at a fixed end of a member are termed **Fixed-end forces**, and the moment, which is of particular interest, is termed the **Fixed-end moment**. The value $qL^2/2$ for the fixed-end moment of a cantilever beam is as significant and widely encountered as the value

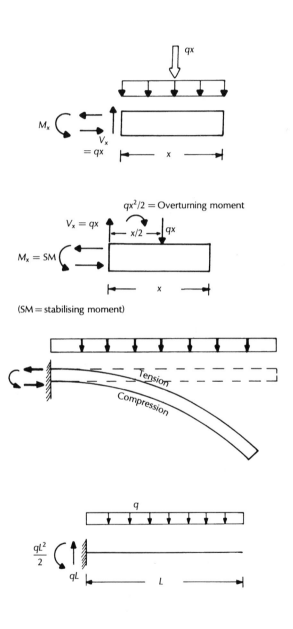

$qL^2/8$ for the moment at the mid point of a simply
supported beam. Note that, while a simply
supported beam loaded downward has its tension
face at the bottom, the tensioned face of a
cantilever similarly loaded is at its top.

4.4 Comments

Apart from their ubiquity, the simply supported
beam and cantilever beam can be considered as
'protostructures'. Practically any terrestrial structure can be considered, on a grand scale, as either
a spanning structure, analogous to a simply
supported beam (e.g. bridges, halls, roofs), or as
a cantilever (tall buildings, towers, masts) or a
combination of the two.

Most structures founded on earth can be considered as bridging a span to support vertical loads
(weight) and cantilevering from earth to support
horizontal loads (wind, earthquake loads). An
understanding of the overall behaviour of such
structures – their stability and the forces they
apply to and receive from their foundations –
can be obtained by reference to the simply supported beam and cantilever models.

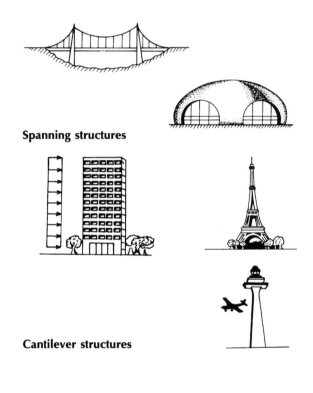

Spanning structures

Cantilever structures

4.5 Moment and shear diagrams

4.5.1 Force diagram

A **Force diagram** is a diagram plotting the
variation of an internal force (axial, shear,
bending moment) along a member. The diagram
is plotted on the line diagram of the member so
that the value of the force is measured perpendicular to the member axis. Force diagrams can
be plotted for whole structures by plotting them
for each member on the line diagram of the
structure.

4.5.1.1 Moment diagram – a diagram of the
bending moment – is of particular interest because of the relation observed in the above

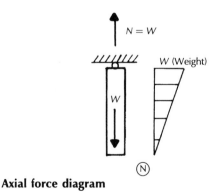

Axial force diagram

examples between the **sense** of the moment, the tension and compression faces, convexity–concavity and therefore deformations in general.

4.5.1.2 Given a moment diagram of a structure, the flow of tensile and compressive forces can be traced through it, and the way it deforms can be plotted. More importantly, if the deformed shape is known, and it is often possible to understand it intuitively (see the examples above in 4.2 and 4.3), it is possible to trace the moment diagram **qualitatively**, without performing a single computation, and thus gain a conceptual under-standing of the behaviour of the structure.

The process of drawing shear and moment diagrams, and the relation between moment diagrams and deformed shapes, are demonstrated below for the beams of examples 1 and 2.

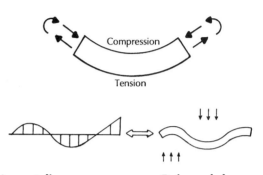

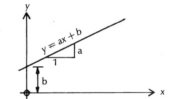

Moment diagram   **Deformed shape**

4.6 Simply supported beam diagrams

4.6.1 Shear diagram

4.6.1.1 The general expression obtained for the shear force in the simply supported beam was (4.2.3): $V_x = qx - qL/2$. Considered as a function with V_x as the dependent variable and x as the independent variable, this is an equation of a straight line. If the usual equation of a straight line in an x–y Cartesian system of axes is

$$y = ax + b,$$

then the substitution

$$y \equiv V_x; \quad a \equiv q; \quad b \equiv -qL/2$$

yields this equation.

4.6.1.2 If we plot the line we can confirm the values computed in the example: the shear forces are (numerically) equal to the reactions at the supports and vanish at mid span.

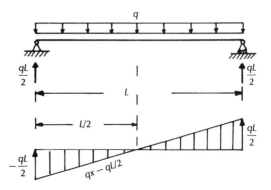

4.6.1.3 The sign of V_x depends on our choice (we chose upward on the free-body diagram from support A) and is not very significant. The nature of the line as a straight line, however, is directly associated with the nature of the load – uniformly distributed load. (This can be verified by following the derivation.) The shear diagram for a UDL is **always** a straight line.

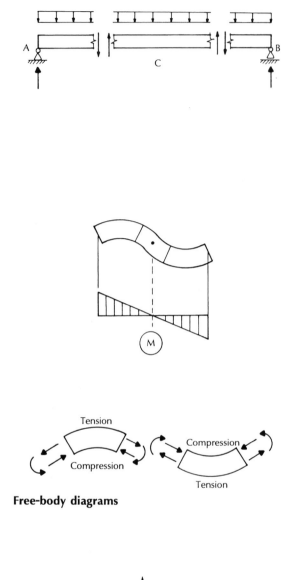

4.6.2 Moment diagram

As mentioned above, moment diagrams are of greater significance than shear diagrams. The first thing to note is the relation between the **sense** of the bending moment (the internal couple) and the tension and compression faces, and hence between the moment and the convexity/concavity (or curvature) of the beam. **A change in the sense of the moment implies and is implied by a change in the curvature of the beam and a switch of the tensioned and compressed sides.**

4.6.2.1 Such change also implies a change in the algebraic sign of the bending moment, but since the algebraic sign depends on an arbitrary choice of a 'positive sense' it is not significant. What is significant is which side is compressed and which tensioned. The moment diagram should reflect this aspect, which is a property of the structure and the load and does not depend on choice of signs.

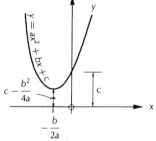

Free-body diagrams

4.6.2.2 The general expression obtained for the bending moment in simply supported beam was: $M_x = -qx^2/2 + qLx/2$. This is the equation of a **parabola**. The equation of a parabola in the x–y Cartesian coordinate system is:

$$y = ax^2 + bx + c$$

The substitution:

$$y \equiv M_x; \quad a \equiv -q/2; \quad b \equiv qL/2; \quad c = 0$$

yields this equation.

4.6.2.3 We noted that M_x is always 'positive' and, more importantly, that the beam does not change curvature – the top side is concave and the bottom side is convex along the whole beam. This implies that **the moment diagram is completely to one side of the line diagram of the beam**.

To which side we draw the diagram is a matter of choice, but it is important that we adopt a consistent convention, since this convention is what will indicate, by looking at the diagram, which side of the beam is in tension and which side is in compression. In this book, the European convention of **drawing the diagram on the tension side** is generally adopted.

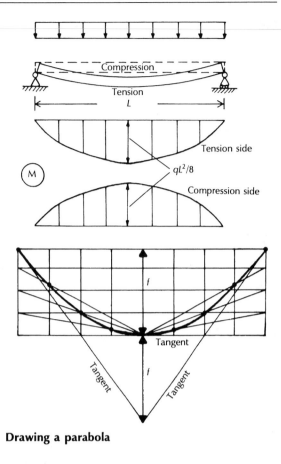

In the USA the diagram is often drawn on the compression side. The reasons for the differences are historical. In Europe, where reinforced concrete is dominant, the tension side is the one where the main reinforcement should be put and the moment diagram serves to highlight this side (see 6.2.2). In the USA steel is (or used to be) the dominant construction material and the compressive side, subject to lateral buckling (7.2.3), is more critical in design.

Drawing a parabola

4.6.2.4 As in the case of the shear diagram, the nature of the moment diagram – a parabola – is derived from the nature of the load (uniformly distributed load). Note also the relation between the direction of the load and the curvature of the parabola. (Think of an umbrella, where the shaft, from handle to tip, indicates the direction of the load, and the ribs or surface, the moment diagram.)

4.6.2.5 Knowing the facts listed below enables the complete drawing of the diagram with minimal computation:

❏ The moment at the supports vanishes (hinged supports).
❏ The moment at mid span is $qL^2/8$.
❏ The tension (convex) side is at the bottom.
❏ The moment diagram is a parabola.

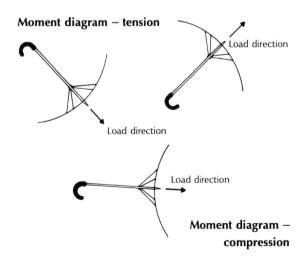

Moment diagram – tension

Moment diagram – compression

4.7 Cantilever beam – moment diagram

We can draw the moment diagram of the cantilever beam based on the following information:

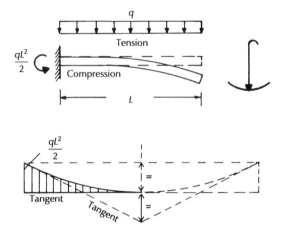

❏ The moment at the free end is zero.
❏ The moment at the fixed end is $qL^2/2$.
❏ The tension side is at the top.
❏ The moment diagram is a parabola.
❏ The curvature of the parabola relates to the
   direction of the load like the ribs (or surface) of
   an umbrella to its shaft.
❏ The diagram at the free end is tangent to the
   base line. This is a result of the vanishing of the
   shear and is given here without proof.

The shear force function is the derivative of the
moment function and hence indicates the slope.
Where the shear vanishes the slope is zero and the
tangent to the curve is parallel to the x axis.

Note that the cantilever parabola is exactly half of a
simply supported beam parabola with the span
doubled and the parabola shifted to the top
$(qL^2/2 = q(2L)^2/8)$.

4.8 Example 3: truss

4.8.1 Definition

Truss
A bar structure in which bars are subject to axial
action only (at least to a reasonable approximation). There is no shear force and no bending
moment in any of the bars. From the analytical
point of view the bar is idealised to be pin-ended,
i.e. the joints are assumed to be frictionless pin
joints, and the load is assumed to be applied to the
truss as concentrated point loads at the joints only
(otherwise the bars would be subject to bending).

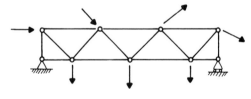

Truss

4.8.1.1 It follows from the definition of truss (pin joints and no load along members) that not only are bars subjected only to axial forces, but that the axial force is constant along the bar (since no new force is introduced at any point between the joints along the bar). It also follows from the definition that trusses cannot have fixed supports, only hinged supports or rollers (since the support is one of the joints).

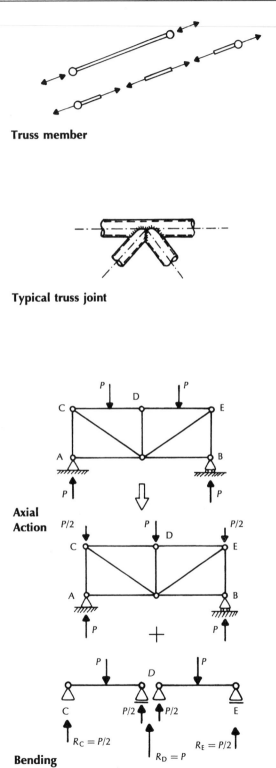

Truss member

Typical truss joint

4.8.1.2 In practice, the joints are often executed as rigid (e.g. by welding), but the analysis is performed as though they were pinned. The error in the analysis, however, is small since bending moments due to joint rigidity in trusses are negligible in most cases.

What makes a truss act primarily through axial forces is not the nature of the joints, but the geometry of the structure. **Planar trusses** typically consist of a triangular network of bars, but this is not always the case (see Chapter 7 for conditions of stability and rigidity of pin-jointed networks). The general rule is that if it is possible for a bar structure to act as a truss (i.e. possible to maintain equilibrium in axial action alone), it will. **Axial action takes precedence over flexure** (see *Direct action*, 7.6.2).

4.8.1.3 The restriction that no loads are applied along members is often not complied with in practice. In cases where loads are applied along a member of a truss, this member is subjected to bending in addition to the axial force. If the structure as a whole has a truss layout, the two effects can be separated in the analysis. First, loads are concentrated at the joints and the truss, as a whole, is analysed to compute axial forces (see the following example). The bending moments in those members loaded along their length are then computed by considering them as beams supported at the joints.

4.8.1.4 The fact that the primary action in a truss is axial is of major influence, both on simplifying the analysis and, more importantly, on the efficiency and weight of the structure (Chapter 5).

4.8.2 Data

Given: a plane truss of the geometry shown, loaded as shown.

Required: the (axial) forces in the bars, and the reaction forces.

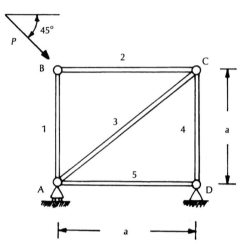

4.8.3 Solution

4.8.3.1 General
This simple truss can be considered as both simply supported and cantilever configuration (see 4.4). The analysis of a simply supported configuration typically starts with computing the reactions. The analysis of a cantilever configuration starts at the free end, and reactions are computed at the end. As demonstrated in the beam examples, cantilever analysis is somewhat simpler. Its application follows.

4.8.3.2 Truss analysis can be made more systematic than beam analysis. The typical free-body diagram in a full truss analysis is a single joint with the member ends joining it.

In a planar truss joint there are two equilibrium equations for the sums of forces in the x and y directions:

$$\sum (P_x) = 0; \qquad \sum (P_y) = 0$$

In a spatial truss joint there is a third equation for forces in the z direction. The moment equation is automatically satisfied by the truss definition (pinned joints, loads at joints only). Consequently any joint free-body diagram in a plane truss can yield at most two unknown member forces. It is customary to number or otherwise identify joints and members to assist in the procedure.

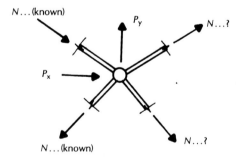

Truss joint as free-body diagram

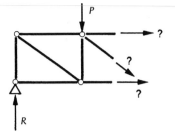

The forces in specific members can be computed by different free-body diagrams. For instance, the free-body diagram can be a segment of the truss between a support (or free end) and a cross-section through the member(s) in question. In this case, the third equation – vanishing of the moment – comes into play. This 'method of sections' is useful when not all member forces are required.

4.8.3.3 Step 1

Look for a joint (other than a support) at which only two members meet. If there is one, start the analysis there (joint B in the present case). If there is not, compute reactions and start at a support joint with two members.

'Cut' the members joining at the node near the joint and draw a free-body diagram of the joint, showing all applied loads and member forces, including unknown forces. **Show unknown forces as tension forces** (pointing away from the joint). **Axial tension forces are considered positive.**

4.8.3.4 Compute up to two member forces from equilibrium equations ('right' and 'up' are considered positive). The applied load is first replaced by its Cartesian components (2.6). For the given loads the components are: $P_x = P/\sqrt{2}$ and $P_y = -P/\sqrt{2}$. The equilibrium equations then yield:

$$\sum(P_x) = 0 \Rightarrow P/\sqrt{2} + N_2 = 0$$
$$\Rightarrow N_2 = -P/\sqrt{2}(\leftarrow)$$
$$\sum(P_y) = 0 \Rightarrow -P/\sqrt{2} - N_1 = 0$$
$$\Rightarrow N_1 = -P/\sqrt{2}(\uparrow)$$

The indices of member forces refer to member numbers.

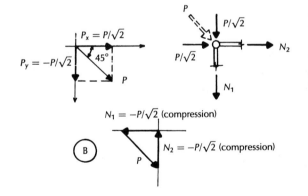

4.8.3.5 In cases like the present, where members form regular angles with one another, it is often easier to compute forces by a semi-graphic method, employing the **closed force polygon**

formed by forces at the node (3.1.1). The result is obtained directly from the geometry of the polygon (triangle in this case). Note that the arrows of the force vectors **relate to the node**, so an arrow pointing towards the node (as all arrows in this case are) indicates compression (and therefore 'negative') force, and an arrow pointing away from the joint indicates tension (and therefore 'positive') force.

4.8.3.6 Step 2
Proceed to the next joint in which there are no more than two, as yet unknown, forces – joint C in the present case. Repeat the procedure of step 1. Show the known forces, including those previously computed in their correct direction. For instance, N_2 is compression and therefore acts **towards** the joint. Show unknown forces as tension forces (away from the joint). Compute the unknown forces, either analytically or by using the geometry of the force polygon.

4.8.3.7 Following steps
Continue in the same manner through all the joints. Reactions are computed as part of the process, in the present case.

Reactions may have to be computed from equilibrium of the whole truss – similar to the simply supported beam example – if in the computation process no joint can be found with only two unknown forces. Note that in the equilibrium equations for the whole truss (as opposed to that of a single joint) moment equation(s) do feature, as the truss as a whole is a rigid body, not free to rotate.

4.8.3.8 Final check
At the end of the process there is always a possibility of checking the results. The check can be at a joint where only one force is unknown or where all forces have been computed and equilibrium can be checked. In the present case,

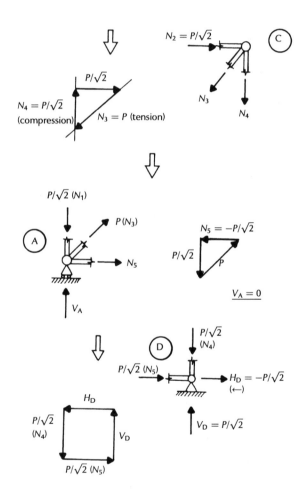

equilibrium of the truss as a whole can be used to check the reactions computed:

$$\sum (P_x) = 0 \Rightarrow H_D + P/\sqrt{2} = 0$$
$$\Rightarrow H_D = -P/\sqrt{2}(\leftarrow)$$
$$\sum (P_y) = 0 \Rightarrow V_A + V_B - P/\sqrt{2} = 0$$
$$\Rightarrow V_A + V_B = P/\sqrt{2}$$

The vanishing of the reaction force V_A can be observed by considering rotation of the truss around support B. All forces on the truss except V_A (namely P, H_A, V_B) pass through point B and therefore do not produce couples relative to B. There is therefore no overturning moment and the stabilising moment produced by V_A (and lever arm a) must vanish.

4.8.4 Presentation of results

It is customary to present a summary of the results on a line diagram of the truss. On each member the axial force in the member is written (with + sign for tension and − sign for compression). All applied loads and reaction forces are also shown. Member forces can be shown as well as arrows on the member. The arrows **relate to the joint**. A member, the arrows of which point to the joints, is in compression. If the arrows point into the member, the member is in tension (it 'pulls' on the joint).

4.8.5 Conclusion

It can be concluded from the computation process that **the total number of equilibrium equations available in a plane truss is twice the number of joints**. This result is used in subsequent sections, relating to the *stability* and *rigidity* of pin-jointed networks (7.5).

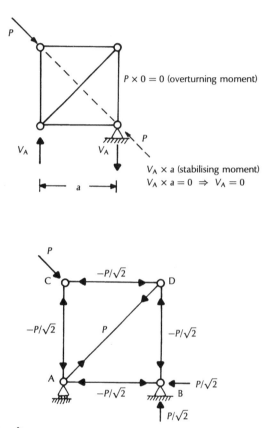

Results

5 Force–Displacement Relations in Structures

5.1 Statics

Statics

Relations between forces in equilibrium. Equilibrium equations are also termed 'equations of statics'.

5.1.1 Static determinacy

5.1.1.1 Structures of the kind analysed in the preceding chapter, where there are just enough equilibrium equations to compute all the forces in the structure (reaction and internal forces), are termed *Statically determinate* structures.

5.1.1.2 Many structures, however, are not of this type. For instance, a *Propped cantilever* is a beam with a fixed support at one end and a roller at the other end, having four reaction components. Similarly, a planar truss may not possess a joint in which only two members meet. Such structures are termed *Statically indeterminate* or *Statically redundant* structures.

The concepts of *Static determinacy* and *Static redundancy* are fundamental concepts in structural engineering.

The term 'indeterminacy' indicates (somewhat negatively, perhaps) that there are not enough equilibrium equations (equations of statics) to resolve the forces. The term 'redundancy' (looking on the bright side) refers to there being more components (supports and/or members) than are required to maintain equilibrium. These 'redundant' components could be removed without loss of stability (although they may perform functions other than maintaining stability).

Propped cantilever

Statically indeterminate   **Statically determinate**

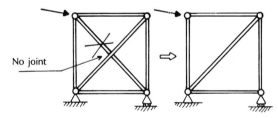

Statically indeterminate truss

No joint

How are forces (internal and reaction forces) to be computed in statically indeterminate structures? Clearly, equilibrium is not the only condition required of a structure, and other conditions may affect the nature and magnitude of forces.

5.2 Kinematics

Kinematics
Relations among displacements or deformations in a structure. Certain conditions need to be satisfied by displacements and deformations for a structure to maintain its integrity and fulfill its function.

5.2.1 *Compatibility*

Compatibility
The conditions of compatibility include two groups – conditions on displacements and conditions on deformations.

5.2.1.1 Conditions on displacements are employed in the context of redundancy of reaction forces. They state that the displacements at supports must comply with the support conditions – restrained displacements must vanish. For instance, at a hinged support there is no horizontal or vertical displacement; at a roller there is no displacement perpendicular to the direction of rolling, and so on. These types of compatibility conditions are termed ***Boundary conditions***.

Sometimes displacements are not fully restrained. For example, if the support is a spring which only partially restrains displacement, or if a support 'settles', i.e. displaces by a given amount. In these cases as well the displacements have to satisfy certain conditions – a constant proportion between reaction and displacement (the spring 'constant') in the first instance, a prescribed displacement in the second.

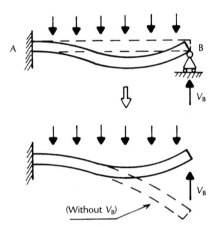

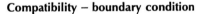

Compatibility – boundary condition

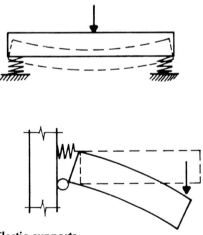

Elastic supports

5.2.1.2 Conditions on deformations, namely on relative displacements of points along members or other components of the structure, are used in dealing with redundancy of internal forces (or of members). The requirement is for *Continuity* of the member or structural component at every point.

The type of continuity required by continuity conditions corresponds to the type of internal force in question and the related deformation. Axial continuity, for instance, requires that there is no gap or overlap along a member's axis. Shear continuity requires that there is no abrupt shearing at a point, and flexural continuity requires that there is no 'break' – a sudden discontinuity, similar to the formation of a hinge where none exists.

5.3 Constitutive relations

In order to use compatibility conditions to compute internal forces and reactions in statically indeterminate structures, we need to be able to relate displacements and deformations to forces. Relations between forces or other static parameters (see *Stress* below) and displacements or other kinematic parameters (see *Strain* below) are termed *Constitutive relations*. As the term implies, these relations are a function of the 'constitution' of the structure, i.e. the properties of the **material** it is made of and other properties of its constituents.

5.3.1 Stiffness

For most conventional building materials (see material properties in Chapter 6), the relation between force and deformation is linear over a large range of the deformation. This linear relation at the material level often translates to a linear relation between forces and displacements at the structural level. The relation between forces

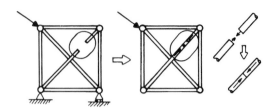

Compatibility – axial continuity

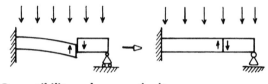

Compatibility – shear continuity

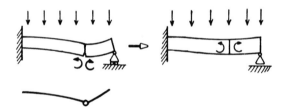

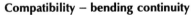

Compatibility – bending continuity

(P) and deformations or displacements (Δ) can therefore be expressed as:

$$P = K \times \Delta$$

where K is the constant of the equation and is termed the *Stiffness* coefficient. Clearly, the larger the value of K, the smaller the deformation or displacement due to a given force and the 'stiffer' the structure. The stiffness coefficient can be defined as the **force required to produce a unit displacement**:

$$K \equiv P|_{\Delta=1}$$

The value of the coefficient varies with the location and direction of the force and displacement in question.

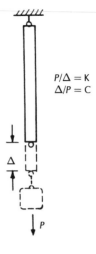

$P/\Delta = K$
$\Delta/P = C$

5.3.2 Flexibility

If we express the displacement as a function of the force, we get the inverse relation:

$$\Delta = C \times P \qquad (C = 1/K)$$

where C is the constant of the equation. In the case where the two expressions relate to the same force and displacement, C is the inverse of K. It is, accordingly, termed the *Flexibility* coefficient. The flexibility coefficient is the **displacement produced by a unit force**:

$$C \equiv \Delta|_{P=1}$$

When the equations above relate to more than one force and displacement acting simultaneously, the parameters P and Δ represent 'vectors' (in the mathematical, not the physical sense), and the co-efficients K and C are 'matrices'.

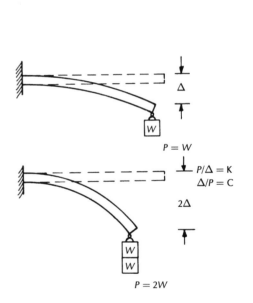

$P = W$

$P/\Delta = K$
$\Delta/P = C$

2Δ

$P = 2W$

5.4 Analysis – force method

The formulation of constitutive relations for a structure implies the establishment of the relation between any force in the structure (external or internal) and any displacement or deformation, namely, the computation of the appropriate stiffness or flexibility coefficient. The general formulation of such relations is beyond the scope of this book (it requires proficiency in calculus).

The following is an outline of the general procedure for employing flexibility constitutive relations and compatibility conditions in the computation of forces in statically indeterminate structures.

5.4.1 Step by step procedure

5.4.1.1 Step 1: the released structure

'Release' as many **Redundant forces** as necessary to make the structure statically determinate – the **Released structure**. Which forces are considered 'redundant', and consequently the nature of the released structure, is to a large extent a matter of choice.

For example, a propped cantilever could be released into a cantilever by releasing the roller reaction, or into a simply supported beam by releasing the fixed-end moment.

Releasing a force means removing a restraint **corresponding** to that force. The term 'corresponding' means that the 'movement' (displacement or deformation) facilitated by the release is exactly in the direction (degree of freedom) the force is trying to cause the structure (or member) to move.

If the redundant force is a reaction, then releasing it means altering the nature of the support in such a way that there are fewer reaction components – turning a fixed support into a hinged one, a hinged support into a roller or removing a roller.

If the redundant force is an internal force, releasing the corresponding degree of freedom means introducing a discontinuity of the sort discussed above (5.2.1.2). Such release is more difficult to visualise.

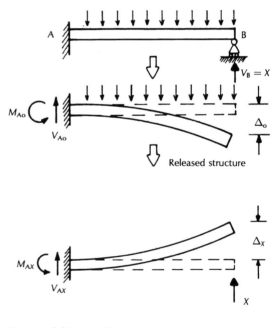

Released structure

Compatibility condition:

$$\Delta_B = \Delta_o + \Delta_X = 0 \Rightarrow$$

$$\Delta_o + CX = 0 \Rightarrow X = -\frac{\Delta_o}{C}$$

$$V_A = V_{Ao} + V_{AX}; \qquad M_A = M_{Ao} + M_{AX}$$

5.4.1.2 Step 2: the released displacements

(a) Compute the displacements (or deformations) corresponding to the redundant forces, under the applied load, in the released structure, using flexibility constitutive relations.

(b) Compute the displacements (or deformations) corresponding to the redundant forces, in the released structure under the action of a unit value of each of the redundant forces, one at a time. By the definition (5.3.2), these are flexibility coefficients.

5.4.1.3 Step 3: compatibility conditions

Compute the values of the redundant forces, such that the corresponding displacements (deformations) vanish, under the combined action of the applied loads and the redundant forces. The resulting **equations of compatibility** are a set of simultaneous linear equations with the redundant forces as the unknowns, the flexibility coefficients (5.4.1.2b) as the coefficients of the equations, and the computed displacements under the applied load (5.4.1.2a) as the right hand side (with inverted signs).

5.4.1.4 Step 4: computation of forces

Having computed the redundant forces from the equations of compatibility, all other forces (reactions and internal) can be computed by treating the redundant forces as external loads (in addition to the given loads) **on the released – statically determinate** structure.

5.4.1.5 Notes

(a) All the computations are performed on the released, statically determinate structure, and therefore all forces can be computed from equilibrium conditions.

(b) The compatibility conditions for redundant reaction forces are boundary conditions. The compatibility condition for internal redundant forces are continuity conditions.

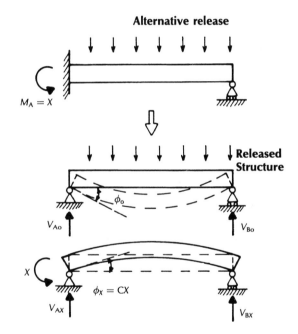

Alternative release

$M_A = X$

Released Structure

V_{Ao} V_{Bo} ϕ_o

X $\phi_x = CX$ V_{AX} V_{BX}

Compatibility condition:

$$\varphi_A = \varphi_0 + \varphi_X = 0$$

$$\varphi_0 + CX = 0 \Rightarrow X = -\frac{\varphi_0}{C} = M_A$$

$$V_A = V_{Ao} + V_{AX}; \qquad V_B = V_{Bo} + V_{BX}$$

The concepts of stiffness and flexibility form the basis of the two main methods of structural analysis – the **flexibility method** (also termed 'force method' or 'compatibility method') is the method outlined above. It is based on computing redundant forces from **compatibility equations**, with flexibility coefficients forming the coefficients for the set of equations.

The **stiffness method** (also termed 'displacement method' or 'equilibrium method') uses the stiffness formulation to express the equilibrium equations, not in terms of forces, but in terms of displacements, as the unknown variables. Stiffness coefficients form the coefficients of the set of equilibrium equations. These equations express the relation between the external loads, assumed to act at the nodes, and the displacements of the nodes. Once displacements are computed, internal forces can be computed using the stiffness relations of individual members. This method is less intuitive than the flexibility method, but it is more rigorous computationally, and more convenient for implementation by computers.

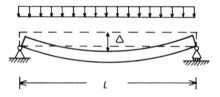

5.5 Factors affecting stiffness and flexibility

Although a quantitative derivation of stiffness and flexibility coefficients is beyond the scope of this book, a conceptual understanding of factors affecting these parameters is essential for the understanding of the behaviour of structures.

Looking at a simple structure, such as a simply supported beam or a cantilever, it is possible to write an intuitive expression for the factors affecting the *Deflection* of the beam:

Deflection is the displacement at a specific location due to a given load. Usually the maximum displacement is sought. In the case of the simply supported beam it would be the displacement at mid span. The terms 'displacement' and 'deflection' are often used interchangeably.

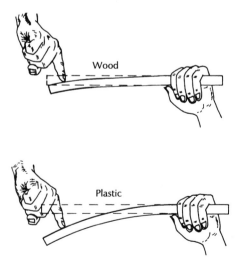

The 'intuitive expression' for the deflection can be written as a fraction, with factors increasing deflection in the nominator and factors decreasing it in the denominator:

$$\Delta = \left\{ \text{constant} \; \frac{\text{span (length)}}{(\text{material stiffness}) \times (\text{cross-section dimensions})} \right\} \times \text{load}$$

The expression in braces lists factors affecting the flexibility coefficient C. Clearly, the deflection increases with the span. On the other hand, stiffer material and larger cross-section decrease the deflection.

Following is a somewhat more detailed discussion of the two denominator factors – material and cross-section.

5.5.1 Material stiffness

The stiffness of a material is determined by performing a loading test on a specimen made from the material, and measuring the load and the deformations.

The usual test is a tension loading of a specimen in the shape of a strip or rod with a cross-sectional area A (mm^2). The specimen is pulled in a testing machine. The tension force T (Newtons) is measured, as well as the elongation ΔL (mm) of a segment of the specimen, whose initial length is L (mm).

The coefficient of stiffness of the material – the *Modulus of elasticity* or *Elastic modulus* – is defined in terms which are independent of the dimensions of the specimen:

$$E = \frac{(T/A)}{(\Delta L/L)}$$

The modulus of elasticity, E, also known as Young's modulus (Thomas Young, 1773–1829), is in units of force/length^2 (N/mm$^2 \equiv$ MPa – Mega-Pascals). A more detailed discussion of the mechanical properties of materials is given in Chapter 6.

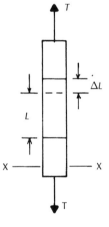

$A = b \times t$

Cross-section X–X

$$E = \frac{T/A}{\Delta L/L}$$

The parameter in the nominator – (T/A) – is termed *stress*, the parameter in the denominator – ($\Delta L/L$) – is *strain*. See 5.7 below.

5.5.2 *Moment of inertia*

The influence of the dimensions of the cross-section on the stiffness is intuitively apparent, but the different dimensions (width, height etc.) do not influence the deflection in the same way. This influence is of subtle and major significance for structural behaviour as a whole.

5.5.2.1 To demonstrate the differing influence of dimensions, perform the following experiment. Get a ruler or other strip of material with width considerably greater than thickness. Place it on two supports in a simply supported beam fashion, and load it at the centre of the span. First load it when it is lying on its width (that is loaded in its thickness direction). Next load it 'standing on edge' (loaded in its width direction). The difference in deflection is apparent.

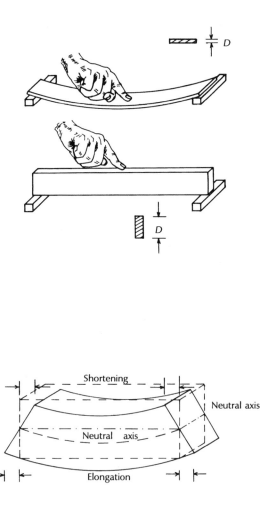

5.5.2.2 It can be seen that increasing the dimension in the loading direction – the **depth** – has a much larger influence on reducing the deflection than increasing the dimension perpendicular to the plane of loading – the width.

As observed previously (Chapter 4), the top face of the beam contracts and the bottom face elongates. Since the two faces are connected by the continuum of material, there must be a surface across the depth of the beam which neither contracts nor elongates. This surface runs along the beam and across its width.

The line this surface forms along the beam axis, or across the cross-section is termed the ***Neutral axis***. The line along the beam is the neutral axis of the beam, whereas the line across the cross-section is the neutral axis of the cross-section.

5.5.2.3 For symmetric cross-sections, like the rectangular cross-section considered above, it is natural to assume that the neutral axis is at the centre – midway between top and bottom faces. In general, the neutral axis passes through the *Centre of gravity* (or *Centroid*) of the cross-section.

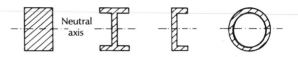

Symmetric cross-sections

The **Centre of gravity** or **Centroid** of a cross-section is defined through the parameter termed **First moment of area**. The first moment of area of a small particle of the cross-section with respect to a line is defined as the area of the particle, a, multiplied by its distance from the line, y. If the line passes through the cross-section then y is defined positive to one side of the line and negative to the other side. The first moment of area of the whole section with respect to the line is the algebraic sum of the first moments of area of all the particles.

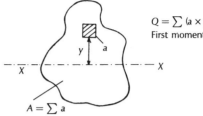

$$Q = \sum (a \times y)$$
First moment of area

This is an approximate definition, bypassing the need to resort to calculus. It would become accurate only when the particle's area a becomes negligibly small (infinitesimal). The summation operation then is termed 'integration'.

The centre of gravity is a point in the cross-section having the property that the first moment of area of the cross-section vanishes, with respect to any line passing through this point. Any axis of symmetry of a cross-section passes through the centre of gravity. The locations of centres of gravity of commonly used cross-sections are given in tables in the technical literature. An empirical procedure for deriving it is given below.

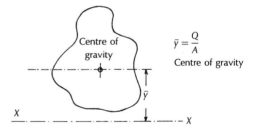

$$\bar{y} = \frac{Q}{A}$$
Centre of gravity

The relation of the neutral axis to the centre of gravity is a result of equilibrium of the internal forces. For the two forces forming the internal couple to be equal, the first moment of area of the tension and compression parts of the cross-section with respect to the neutral axis must be equal. See discussion of *stress* in 5.7 below.

5.5.2.4 The significant influence of the cross-section dimension, then, is not the total amount of material but **the location of material with respect to the neutral axis**. The further material is spread away from the neutral axis in the direction of the load, the stiffer the member.

The parameter which expresses the distribution of material with respect to the neutral axis is the *Moment of inertia*, or the *Second moment of area* of the cross-section. Its definition is as follows:

The moment of inertia of a small particle of the cross-section whose area is a and whose distance from the neutral axis in the loading direction (perpendicular to the neutral axis) is y is defined as $a \times y^2$. The moment of inertia of the whole cross-section is obtained by summing up the moments of inertia of all such particles over the cross-section. Moments of inertia of commonly used cross-sections are given in tables in the technical literature.

Empirical determination of moment of inertia of an arbitrary cross-section.

(1) Cut from cardboard a scaled model of the cross-section and paste graph paper on it.

(2) Hang the model at a point close to its circumference and, with the help of a plumb (a weight tied to a string) draw a vertical line across the model from this point.

(3) Repeat step (2) using a different point. The intersection of the two lines drawn across the cross-section is the **centre of gravity**.

(4) Draw a line perpendicular to the direction of load through the centre of gravity – the **neutral axis**.

(5) Fill in a square of desired size (depending on the precision wanted) of area a and measure and write its distance from the neutral axis.

(6) Repeat step (5) for all squares (of identical size).

(7) Perform the calculation:

$$I = \frac{a \sum (y^2)}{\text{scale}^4} \equiv \text{Moment of inertia}$$

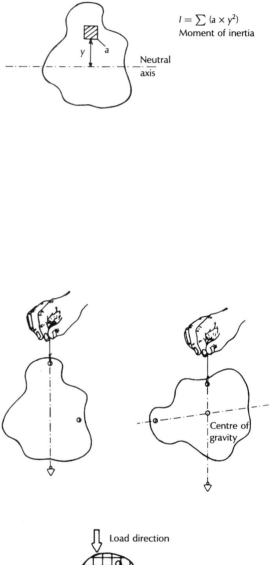

$$I = \sum (a \times y^2)$$
Moment of inertia

Neutral axis

Centre of gravity

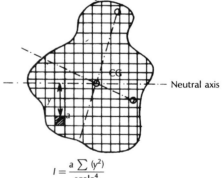

Load direction

Neutral axis

$$I = \frac{a \sum (y^2)}{\text{scale}^4}$$

5.5.3 *Deflections of beams*

The deflection at mid span of a simply supported beam loaded with a uniformly distributed load q is given by:

$$\Delta = \frac{5qL^4}{384EI}$$

where I is the moment of inertia of the cross-section.

The deflection at the end of a cantilever similarly loaded is:

$$\Delta = \frac{qL^4}{8EI}$$

Values for other beams and other loading conditions can be found in tables in the technical literature.

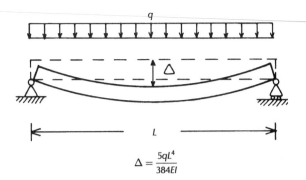

$$\Delta = \frac{5qL^4}{384EI}$$

5.6 Structural efficiency

As seen above, material close to the neutral axis contributes little to the stiffness of a beam. It also contributes little to the *capacity* of the beam.

The **Capacity** of a beam is the maximum internal moment the beam is capable of sustaining to resist load. Naturally, it depends on the strength of the material, which determines the maximum magnitude of the forces in the internal couple (see Chapter 6).

Given a specific material, the capacity is determined by the **lever arm** of the internal couple. Obviously, material close to the neutral axis contributes little to the lever arm. The further away from the neutral axis the material is concentrated, the larger the internal couple lever arm, and the stronger and stiffer the structure.

This is the reason that steel beams are usually not made as rectangular sections but with most of the material concentrated in *flanges* away from the neutral axis. The thin *web* serves to connect the flanges and sustain the shear forces (see example in 6.3.2).

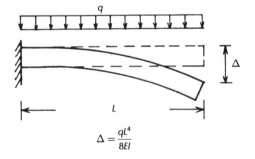

$$\Delta = \frac{qL^4}{8EI}$$

5.6.1 Structural depth

The **Structural depth** of a structure or component is the lever arm of the stabilising moment, when the equilibrium of the structure or component is considered (see Chapter 4). From this definition it is clear that the structural depth depends on the free-body diagram being considered, and that it varies over the structure. This is, arguably, the most important concept in structural engineering. Understanding structural depth and its variation over the structure implies understanding the structure's equilibrium and the flow of internal forces.

5.6.2 Material dilution

Dilution of material consists of increasing structural depth without increasing the amount of material (and hence the weight of the structure). In fact, dilution of material reduces its total amount, since increasing structural depth reduces the magnitude of the internal forces, under given loads, and therefore the amount of material required to resist them (see example in 6.3.2).

5.6.3 Shape and structural efficiency

5.6.3.1 Structural efficiency is defined as the ratio of the load-bearing capacity to the weight of the structure.

This concept is directly related to structural depth, since the larger the structural depth, the larger the load-bearing capacity (strength) of the structure or alternatively, the less material is required to support a given load.

In practice, there is a limit beyond which increasing structural depth results in an increase in weight (see 6.3.2). This limit is the optimal structural depth, from the structural efficiency viewpoint. Some rough guidelines for optimal structural depth of various structural systems are given in subsequent chapters.

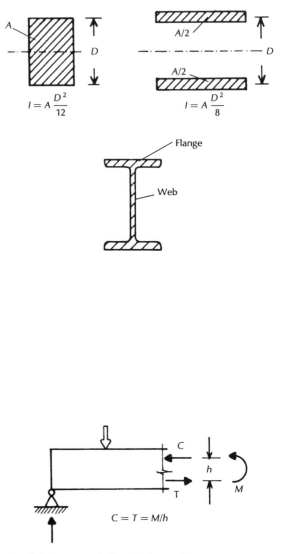

$$I = A\frac{D^2}{12} \qquad I = A\frac{D^2}{8}$$

$$C = T = M/h$$

Small h (structural depth), low stiffness

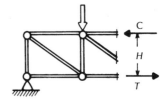

Large structural depth, high stiffness, less material

5.6.3.2 Structural depth of a structure depends to a large extent on the shape and geometry of the structure. The lever arm available for the stabilizing moment at any cross-section through the structure cannot exceed the overall dimensions of the structure. There is, therefore, a close relationship between the **geometry** of a structure and the concepts of **structural depth, structural efficiency, stiffness, displacements** and **forces**.

Efficient structural design consists of selecting and utilising the geometry to maximise structural depth.

The central theme of the second part of the book consists of demonstrating ways in which this principle can be put into effect.

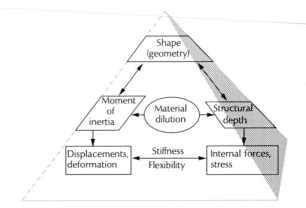

5.7 Stress and strain

In order to understand the way forces 'flow' through the structure's components and the way the material responds to forces, it is necessary to enter the 'microscopic' level of the structural member. It is not enough to consider the member as a whole, or a whole cross-section through the member

5.7.1 Stress

It may be instructive to consider the member as consisting of **fibres**. The internal forces in a cross-section are distributed over all the fibres. If each fibre has a small cross-section area then the force in it divided by its cross-section area is termed the *Stress* in the fibre. Stress has dimensions of force/length^2 (Newton/sq mm – N/mm^2 – Mega-Pascal – MPa).

> This is another approximate definition bypassing calculus. In fact, the stress is the derivative of the internal force with respect to the cross-section area.

5.7.1.1 We have encountered two types of internal forces: *Normal forces* – forces perpendicular

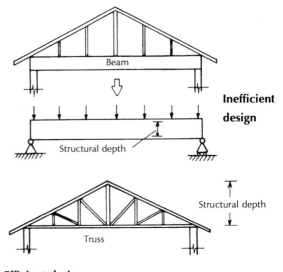

Inefficient design

Efficient design

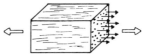

Normal stress

Detail of fibres

to the cross-section, such as axial force and
the forces of the internal couple – and shear
forces – forces in the cross-section surface (perpendicular to the member's axis). Accordingly
there are two types of stresses: **Normal stress** acts
perpendicular to the fibre's cross-section (that is
along the fibre's axis); **Shear stress** acts within the
fibre's cross-section (perpendicular to the fibre's
axis). Normal stresses have the effect of stretching
or shrinking the fibres. Shear stresses try to 'skew'
them – move the tips sideways relative to the
member axis.

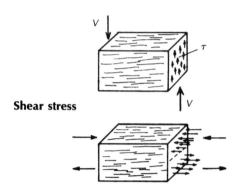

Shear stress

Normal stress in bending

5.7.1.2 Stress distribution
The way stress is distributed over the cross-section
fibres depends on the nature of the internal force.
The resultant of the forces in all fibres must yield
the internal force (or couple). It is reasonable,
therefore, to assume that an axial force is distributed uniformly over all fibres.

It is also clear that the internal couple forming a
bending moment cannot be distributed uniformly,
since it must pass from tension to compression
through zero (at the neutral axis). It is reasonable,
however, to assume that it passes from tension to
compression as a straight line.

This, in fact, is a result of the basic assumption in
bending that planar sections remain planar, and
from the linear stiffness relation between stress and
strain – see below.

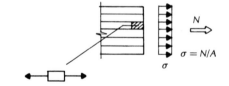

Axial action

$\sigma = N/A$

Distribution of shear stresses over the cross-
section is more complex and will not be dealt
with here. At the surface of the member the stress
must vanish since, generally, there are no external
forces perpendicular to the surface. Equilibrium in
this direction, therefore, requires that no internal
force exists perpendicular to the surface. The shear
stress increases from zero at the surface to a
maximum in the interior, so that the resultant is the
shear force.

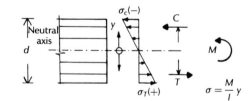

Bending

$\sigma = \dfrac{M}{I} y$

Shear stress differs from normal stress in that it acts not only on the fibre's cross-section, but also along the fibre boundaries, expressing the tendency of fibres to slide relative to one another. If we consider a short length of fibre we see that the shear forces on its parallel cross-section surfaces are of opposing sense (to maintain equilibrium), forming a couple. In order to maintain equilibrium, a couple of opposing sense has to form across the depth of the fibre, producing shear forces on the top and bottom faces of the fibre.

This horizontal shear between fibres can be appreciated in the following simple experiment. Place two or more strips of cardboard or plywood on top of each other and load them in simply supported beam fashion. Observe the strips sliding relative to each other. Now stick pins through both strips at regular intervals and repeat the test. The pins prevent the relative sliding by transmitting the shear forces between the strips. The result is an increase in strength and stiffness due to the increased structural depth. (The strips perform as a single cross-section of full depth.)

5.7.2 *Strain*

In the same way that at the microscopic level of the cross-section the force is distributed over the fibres, the deformations along the member are distributed along the fibres. Each fibre can be perceived of as consisting of links of very small lengths.

Strain is defined as the deformation of a link in the fibre divided by its length. It follows that a strain is dimensionless – length/length (it is measured as %, as 'millistrain' $= 1/1000$, as microstrain $= 10^{-6}$, etc.).

Since strain is the microscopic equivalent of deformation, there must be correspondence between strain and stress. There are, accordingly,

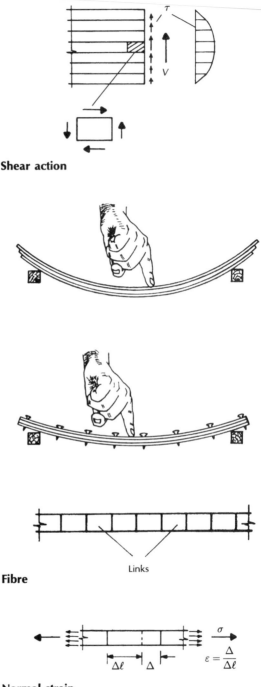

Shear action

Fibre

Links

Normal strain

$$\varepsilon = \frac{\Delta}{\Delta \ell}$$

two types of strain – *Normal strain*, which corresponds to normal stress, and *Shear strain*, which corresponds to shear stress. Normal strain is the elongation of the fibre link divided by its length. Shear strain is the relative lateral movement of the link's ends divided by the link's length. Shear strain is, therefore, an angular parameter, measuring the 'skewing' of the fibre link, namely its deviation from rectangularity.

The distribution of strains over the cross-section is similar to that of stresses, since there is a linear relation between them (see Chapter 6). The variations of both stress and strain along a member are similar to the variation of the internal forces – axial force, bending moment and shear force diagrams.

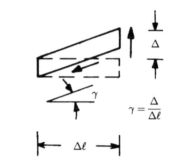

$$\gamma = \frac{\Delta}{\Delta \ell}$$

Shear strain

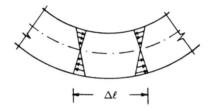

Strain distribution in bending

6 Properties of Materials and Design

6.1 Stress–strain diagrams

As mentioned in Chapter 5 (5.5.1), the main mechanical properties of materials are determined in a
tension test of a specimen. The tensile stress and
strain are measured at regular intervals during the
test (this is done automatically by modern testing
equipment), and a curve is plotted of the stress
versus the strain – the **Stress–strain diagram**. Such
a diagram typically contains several phases. The
main phases are reviewed below, using **Mild steel**
('soft' steel) as a model. Similar phases exist to a
greater or lesser extent in other materials.

6.1.1 Linear elastic phase

At the **Linear elastic** phase the stress–strain diagram forms a straight line. If the load is removed
during this stage both stress and strain return to
zero. **Elasticity** is the property of returning to the
original configuration of stress and strain upon
release of load. **The slope of the straight line is the
elastic modulus:**

$$\sigma = E\varepsilon$$

This, in fact, is the same equation as in 5.5.1,
since:

$$\sigma = T/A; \qquad \varepsilon = \Delta L/L$$

The above relation between stress and strain is
known as **Hooke's Law** (Robert Hooke 1635–
1703). It is a constitutive relation at the material
level and forms the basis for the derivation of
constitutive relations at higher levels (the member,
the structure).

6.1.2 Plastic phase

Beyond the elastic limit, if the load is removed the
stress returns to zero and a **Residual strain** or

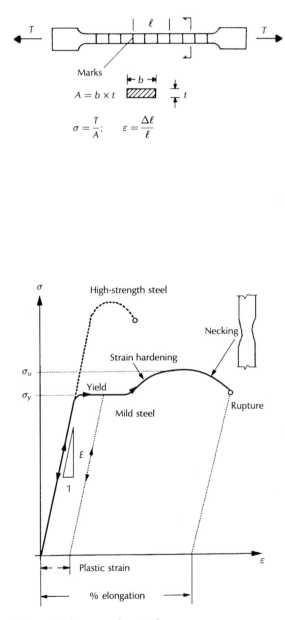

Stress–strain curve for steel

Plastic strain remains. The stress–strain diagram of mild steel contains a region of pure *Plasticity* where strains increase without any significant change in stress. This phenomenon is termed *Yield*, and the stress level at which it occurs is termed *Yield point* or *Yield strength*.

Most materials, such as high-strength steels and other metals, do not possess a clear yield point, but since yield often forms a basis for estimation of strength for design purposes, a nominal yield is defined (usually corresponding to a residual strain of 0.2%).

6.1.3 Strain hardening phase

Following the yield phase there is a phase where stress increases again (though not linearly) with increasing strain. This phase is termed *Strain hardening* (since the material appears to stiffen again following yield). This phase continues until the stress level reaches a peak – the *Ultimate strength*.

6.1.4 Failure phase

Following the ultimate strength the stress appears to decrease with increasing strain up to *Rupture*.

In fact the actual stress does not decrease. Rather, the cross-section area is reduced due to a phenomenon known as *Necking*. Since, however, **nominal** stress is used in the plotting of the diagram – the load divided by the initial cross-section area – the drop in nominal stress reflects the drop in load as cross-section area is reduced.

6.1.5 Ductility and other material properties

The plastic strain remaining after rupture is termed *Per cent elongation* (since it is measured in %). It is a measure of *Ductility*, which is an important property of materials and of structures.

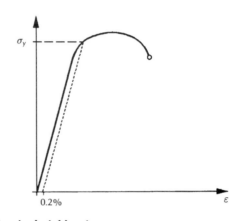

Nominal yield point

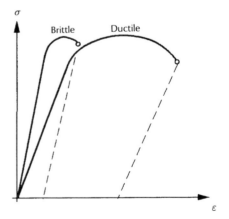

It reflects the ability of the material or structure to sustain deformation without loss of strength. Materials (and structures) with low ductility are termed **Brittle**.

It is possible to draw **force–deflection diagrams** for structures, in a similar manner to stress–strain diagrams. These diagrams express the stiffness, ductility and strength of the structure as a whole.

Other material properties. There is a shear stress–strain diagram associated with materials, similar to the tension one described above. It is difficult to obtain such diagrams experimentally. The shear equivalent of the elastic modulus is the **Shear modulus** or **Modulus of elasticity in shear**, denoted G. Hooke's law for shear is:

$$\tau = G\gamma$$

Another property of materials is that, when the specimen is stretched longitudinally, it also narrows laterally (think of a rubber band being stretched). The ratio between the longitudinal strain and the lateral strain is a material constant known as **Poisson's ratio** (Siméon Denis Poisson 1781–1840). It is denoted μ or ν. Poisson's ratio for mild steel is approximately 0.3.

The three **Elastic constants**, E, G and μ, are not independent but are related through the equation:

$$G = E/[2(1 + \mu)]$$

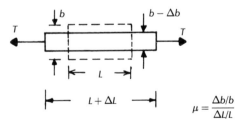

Ductile response

Brittle response

6.2 Properties of common building materials

The main properties of some common building materials are given below for the purpose of comparison. These data are intended to give a rough idea of the comparative properties of these materials. More complete and detailed information can be found in the technical literature.

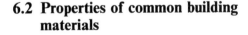

$$\mu = \frac{\Delta b/b}{\Delta L/L}$$

Poisson's ratio

6.2.1 *Steel*

Modulus of elasticity: $E = 205\,000\,\text{N/mm}^2$
Density: $\rho = 7800\,\text{kg/m}^3$.

Mild steel:
Yield strength: $\sigma_y = 200\text{--}350\,\text{N/mm}^2$
Ultimate strength: $\sigma_u = 350\text{--}500\,\text{N/mm}^2$
Per cent elongation: 25–40%

High-strength steel:
Yield strength: $\sigma_y = 350\text{--}600\,\text{N/mm}^2$
  (nominal)
Ultimate strength: $\sigma_u = 450\text{--}1000\,\text{N/mm}^2$
Per cent elongation: 8–22%

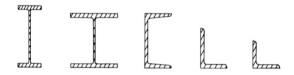

Hot-rolled steel sections

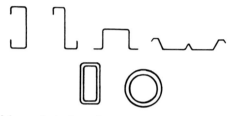

Cold-formed steel sections

6.2.2 *Concrete*

Modulus of elasticity: $E = 20\,000\text{--}40\,000\,\text{N/mm}^2$
  (varies with strength)
Density: $\rho = 2400\,\text{kg/m}^3$
Yield strength: no yield
Ultimate strength in compression
  Ordinary concrete: 20–50 N/mm^2
  High-strength
    concrete: 60–120 N/mm^2
Strength in tension: negligible
Per cent elongation: not applicable (due to
                       lack of tensile strength)

6.2.2.1 Due to the absence of tensile strength, concrete is rarely used as a building material in the pure form. Rather, it is used in combination with steel as *Reinforced concrete*, which is a *Composite material* – a combination of two materials interacting in the transfer of stress and strain.

The main steel reinforcement is placed in regions of tension, for example near the bottom face of simply supported beams or near the top face of cantilever beams.

Additional types of reinforcement include: shear reinforcement, usually in the form of closed *Hoops*

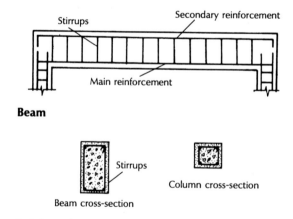

Reinforced concrete

or **Stirrups** or **Ties**, which deal with tensile stress associated with shear (see *Principal stress*, 9.3.2.2); reinforcement for the control cracking, particularly due to temperature effects, *Shrinkage* and *Creep* (see 6.3.3.1 below); non structural reinforcement for construction purposes.

6.2.3 *Wood*

Properties of wood are highly variable, depending on the type of wood and moisture content. The following figures are a rough guide.

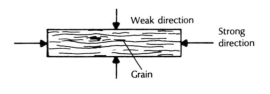

Modulus of elasticity: $E = 7000–16\,000\,\text{N/mm}^2$
Density: $\rho = 400–800\,\text{kg/m}^3$
Yield strength: no yield
Ultimate strength
    parallel to grain: $\sigma_u = 10–20\,\text{N/mm}^2$
    perpendicular to
        grain: $\sigma_u = 1.5–5\,\text{N/mm}^2$
    (compression only)
Per cent elongation: not applicable

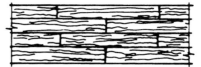

Glued laminated timber (GLULAM)

6.2.4 *Aluminium*

Modulus of elasticity: $E = 70\,000\,\text{N/mm}^2$
Density: $\rho = 2700–2800\,\text{kg/m}^3$
Yield strength
    mild aluminium: $60–120\,\text{N/mm}^2$
    alloy: $200–400\,\text{N/mm}^2$
Per cent elongation: $9–25\%$ (alloy)

Extruded aluminium sections

6.2.5 *Fibre reinforced plastics*

These composite materials are gradually finding their place in the building industries. They consist of synthetic fibres held together by a polymeric matrix. Their properties vary considerably, depending on the type of fibre used, but generally they are characterised by low weight, high strength (parallel to the fibres) and low modulus of elasticity.

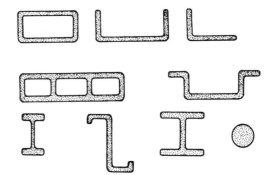

Pultruded fibre reinforced plastic sections

Modulus of elasticity: $E = 50\,000\,\text{N/mm}^2$
(glass fibres) to
$150\,000\,\text{N/mm}^2$
(carbon fibres)

Density: $\rho \cong 2000\,\text{kg/m}^3$

Yield strength: no yield (elastic to rupture)

Ultimate short-term tensile strength
(parallel to fibres): $1500\,\text{N/mm}^2$ (aramid
fibres) to $2000\,\text{N/mm}^2$
(carbon fibres)

Strength perpendicular
to fibres: very low

Long term tensile strength (reduced due
to creep): $800\,\text{N/mm}^2$ (glass) to
$1500\,\text{N/mm}^2$ (carbon)

Per cent elongation: 0%

6.2.6 Comparison table

In the table below, mild steel is used as the yardstick for comparing the material properties of major interest. The figures are approximate averages, for qualitative comparison. The last column gives a relative strength per unit weight of material, which can serve as a measure of structural efficiency at the material level.

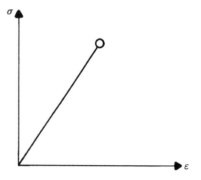

Stress–strain diagram for fibre reinforced plastics

Material	Density ρ	E	Strength σ_u	Stress at service σ_s	σ_s/ρ
Steel					
mild	1	1	1	1	1
high-strength	1	1	2	2	2
Concrete					
normal	0.3	0.15	0.1	0.06	0.2
high-strength	0.3	0.2	0.25	0.15	0.5
Wood	0.075	0.08	0.05	0.06	0.8
Aluminium alloy	0.35	0.33	1	1	3
Fibre reinforced plastics (glass fibres)	0.25	0.25	4.5	2	8

6.3 Some design examples

The design of members in member structures consists of determining the dimensions of the members' cross-sections. The design is based on the computed internal forces in the members, the properties of the materials from which the members are made and on known rules of the behaviour of members under different actions (see Chapters 7 and 8). The detailed procedure of member proportioning forms part of the final design stage (see Chapter 1). Approximate, simplified procedures can be used to estimate member sizes in the preliminary design stage. Both of these stages are beyond the scope of the present work, which is concerned primarily with conceptual design. The examples that follow illustrate the way in which the topics studied in the preceding chapters are combined with knowledge of the properties of the material to arrive at a crude estimate of member sizes under different actions.

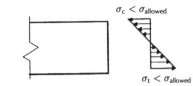

Strength constraints

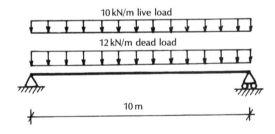

Deflection constraints

6.3.1 Beam design – data

❑ **The beam:** a simply supported beam spanning 10.0 m and supporting a concrete slab.
❑ **Loads:** dead load: 12 kN/m; live load: 10 kN/m. The self weight of the supporting structure (e.g. beam and *slab*) is 7 kN/m.
❑ **Maximum deflection:** the maximum deflection at mid span under the **superimposed load** should not exceed $(1/360) \times 10\,000 = 28$ mm.

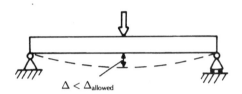

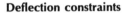

The superimposed load consists of the live load and of a portion of the dead load excluding the self weight of the supporting structure. In this example, therefore, the superimposed load is 15 kN/m. Steel and reinforced concrete alternatives should be considered.

Beam data

A deflection of 1/360 of the span under superimposed load is a typical limiting value specified by codes for concrete slabs.

6.3.2 Steel beam

The beam has an I-shape cross-section. This cross-section consists of two **Flanges** (the top and bottom branches of the I) connected by a **Web** (the stem of the I). This is an efficient cross-section, as it concentrates most of the material in the flanges, away from the neutral axis (see 5.6).

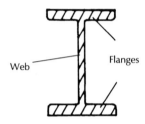

The following simplifying assumptions are adopted:

❏ The material is effectively concentrated in the flanges. The contribution of the web to the stiffness and to the flexural strength is negligible (this is a reasonable first guess assumption).
❏ The material is mild steel with a yield strength of $230 \, \text{N/mm}^2$ and modulus of elasticity of $205\,000 \, \text{N/mm}^2$.
❏ Lateral movement of the compressed flange (the top flange) is restrained – see 7.2.3.2, *Lateral buckling*.

The design involves the determination of two parameters – the depth of the beam and the cross-section area of the flanges. The two parameters are related through the requirements of strength – safety against yielding of the steel, and of serviceability – not exceeding the permissible deflection.

6.3.2.1 Strength
The maximum bending moment at mid span is:

$$M_{max} = qL^2/8 = [(12 + 10)10^2]/8$$

$$= 275 \, \text{kNm} = 275 \times 10^6 \, \text{Nmm}$$

This moment is resisted by the internal force couple which, under the assumptions, is concentrated in the flanges, with a lever arm of h. The values of the compression and tension components

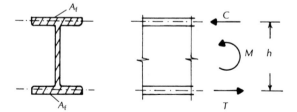

of this couple, C and T, can be obtained from:

$$\sum(F_x) = 0 \Rightarrow C = T;$$
$$T \times h = M = C \times h$$
$$\Rightarrow C = T = M/h = 275 \times 10^6/h$$

The relation between the required depth, h, and the required flange cross-section area, A_f, is obtained from the requirement of safety against yielding of the steel. Assuming a safety factor of 2.0 and assuming the flange forces are uniformly distributed over the flange cross-section, the requirement yields the following relation between h and A_f:

$$C/A_f = T/A_f \le \sigma_y/2.0 = 230/2.0 = 115\,\text{N/mm}^2$$
$$\Rightarrow 275 \times 10^6/(h \times A_f) \le 115$$
$$\Rightarrow h \times A_f \ge 275 \times 10^6/115 = 2.4 \times 10^6\,\text{mm}^3$$

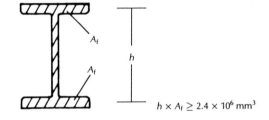

$$h \times A_f \ge 2.4 \times 10^6\,\text{mm}^3$$

6.3.2.2 Serviceability

The deflection at mid span of a simply supported beam loaded by uniformly distributed load is (5.5.3):

$$\Delta = \frac{5qL^4}{384EI}$$

The limitation on deflection under the superimposed load produces another value for the relation between h and A_f. Under the assumption neglecting the web, and assuming a thin flange:

$$I \cong 2 \times A_f(h/2)^2 = h^2 A_f/2$$

Remembering that q in the equation for the deflection relates in the present case to the superimposed load (15 kN/m = 15 N/mm), and converting all units to mm, the additional h–A_f relation is obtained as:

$$\Delta = \frac{5qL^4}{384EI} = \frac{5 \times 15 \times 10\,000^4}{384 \times 205\,000 \times (h^2 A_f/2)}$$
$$= 19 \times 10^9/h^2 A_f \le 28$$
$$\Rightarrow h^2 A_f \ge 6.8 \times 10^8\,\text{mm}^3$$

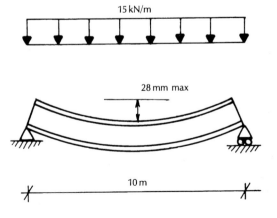

6.3.2.3 Trial sections

Attempting to satisfy the two conditions simultaneously yields the following values for the design parameters:

$$\frac{h^2 A_f}{h A_f} = \frac{6.8 \times 10^8}{2.4 \times 10^6} \Rightarrow h \geq 280 \, \text{mm}$$

$$\Rightarrow A_f \geq 8.6 \times 10^3 \, \text{mm}^2$$

The meaning of these values is that if we adopt a deeper section, we can use a smaller flange and the strength requirement would govern the design (since the moment of inertia increases as the square of the depth, whereas the lever arm only increases linearly). If, on the other hand, a smaller value of the depth is adopted, the deflection requirement would govern. However, it makes no sense to adopt a smaller value for h, since even at the value computed the design is highly inefficient, as is demonstrated by the following table of trial sections. The table is based on actual commercially available profiles, but since details vary among producers, only rough generic properties are given:

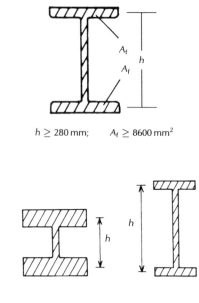

$h \geq 280 \, \text{mm}; \qquad A_f \geq 8600 \, \text{mm}^2$

Low-depth –
deflection governs

High depth –
strength governs

D (mm)	h (mm)	b (mm)	A_f (10^3 mm^2)	hA_f (10^6 mm^3)	$h^2 A_f$ (10^8 mm^4)	W (kg/m)
320	291	305	8.8	2.6	7.5	177
400	376	300	7.2	2.7	11.5	155
440	419	300	6.3	2.6	11.1	140
545	523	212	4.5	2.7	15.8	122
612	592	229	4.5	2.7	15.8	125
678	662	253	4.1	2.7	18.1	125

W is the weight of the beam per 1 m length.

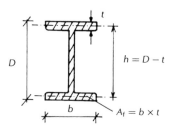

$h = D - t$

$A_f = b \times t$

It can be observed that the weight of the beam, representing efficiency, decreases up to a point with increasing depth, and then starts to rise again. In theory, efficiency should increase with increasing depth, but this is not always expressed in reality. As the beam becomes deeper, more material goes into the web without contributing to strength. Web thickness is controlled by shear (not considered in this example) and by stability requirements (see *Buckling* in Chapter 7). It increases considerably with depth. With special designs and employing the principle of material dilution it is possible to utilise additional depth better (and reduce weight), but even then technical and practical constraints determine the optimal depth.

The optimal depth in the present example is obtained as approximately 1/20 of the span length. This figure is characteristic of a large range of practical cases employing standard profiles and can be adopted as a 'rule of thumb' for such designs. (See Chapter 8 for further rules of thumb for member structures.)

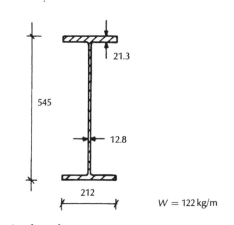

Optimal section

6.3.3 *Concrete beam*

Concrete, being a composite material, is considerably more complex in its behaviour than steel. In addition, it is more difficult to shape it to desired shapes to optimise the cross-section. The following assumptions are made:

❑ The cross-section of the beam is rectangular.
❑ The compressed part of the beam – the top – forms part of a *slab* (8.7), so that compression stress in the concrete is not a limiting constraint.
❑ The centroid of the reinforcing bars at the bottom of the beam is located 50 mm from the bottom face.

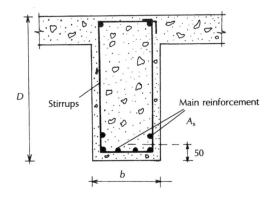

Concrete beam cross-section

The design parameters in this case are the depth of the beam and the amount (cross-section area) of the reinforcement. As in the case of the steel beam, the two parameters are related by the design requirements of strength and serviceability. However, due to the complexity of the material, it is not possible to deal with the two requirements simultaneously in a simple manner, as done in the steel beam example. The depth of concrete beams is usually governed by limitations on deflection.

6.3.3.1 Deflection

The accurate calculation of deflections in reinforced concrete beams is difficult. Due to the
inhomogeneity of the material, the moment of
inertia and the moduli of elasticity of the two
materials forming it are linked. Furthermore,
the moment of inertia varies along the span
because the concrete in the tensile zone is cracked,
and the cracked portion does not contribute to the
stiffness. The extent of cracking varies along
the beam, as it depends on the bending moment.

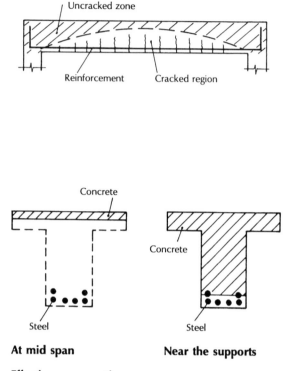

At mid span   Near the supports

Effective cross-section

An additional problem lies in the properties
of **Creep** and **Shrinkage**, which are inherent to
concrete. Concrete shrinks as it hardens (over a
period of one month or more). This shrinkage
causes tensile stresses in the concrete, which leads
to cracking and increased deflection.

Creep is plastic deformation of the concrete
under stress (compression) over time. The deformation is significant and it depends on the stress
level and the quality (strength) of the concrete.
Most of the creep deformation takes place over
the first year or two, provided no additional load
is applied.

Because of these complexities, most design
codes allow a simplified procedure for accounting
for deflections in non exceptional design cases (no
large concentrated forces, cross-section changes
etc.). Deflection requirements are deemed to have
been satisfied provided certain depth/span ratios
are complied with. As a rule of thumb, a depth/
span ratio of 1/10 can be adopted for major
beams of the type considered in the example.

6.3.3.2 Strength

Given the depth and the bending moment
(assumed to be the same as for the steel beam),
it is a simple matter to compute the compression
and tension forces forming the internal couple.
The lever arm is assumed to be 100 mm less than
the depth, i.e. 900 mm:

$$T = M/h = 275 \times 10^6/900 = 306 \times 10^3 \, \text{N}$$

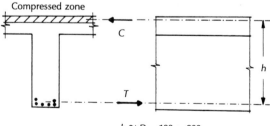

$$h \cong D - 100 = 900$$

The tension force is taken by the reinforcing steel. Typical reinforcing steels have nominal yield strengths of around $400\,\text{N/mm}^2$ and, assuming a safety factor of 2.0, the total cross-section area of the reinforcement is obtained as:

$$A_s = 306\,000/200 = 1530\,\text{mm}^2$$

Various combinations of round bars can satisfy this requirement. (The combinations are given in tables in the technical literature.) For instance, five bars of 20 mm diameter have a cross-section area of $1571\,\text{mm}^2$. These bars are arranged adjacent to the bottom face of the beam and held in position by the stirrups (hoops).

The typical width of concrete beams is $\frac{1}{4}-\frac{1}{3}$ of the depth. The width is determined by requirements for shear capacity, lateral stability and by technical considerations such as accommodation of the reinforcing bars while allowing sufficient space for the concrete to penetrate and cover the bars. Codes specify a minimum thickness of concrete between reinforcing bars and any free surface. This thickness, termed 'cover', is determined by the need for protection of the reinforcement against corrosion, and it varies, depending on exposure conditions. Typical concrete cover is in the range of 20–25 mm.

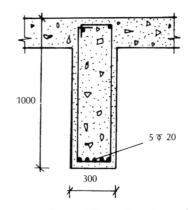

Concrete beam design (dimensions in mm)

6.3.4 Truss – axial action

Data: Design the truss of the example of section 4.8, with the following data: $a = 4.0\,\text{m}$, $P = 50\,\text{kN}$ and the truss members are steel tubes with a yield strength of $230\,\text{N/mm}^2$.

There is a big difference in the behaviour of members acting in tension and those acting in compression. Tension member design is based strictly on the material strength. Compression members are subject to *buckling* (7.2.2) as a failure mode. A bar in compression typically buckles at a stress level which is considerably below the

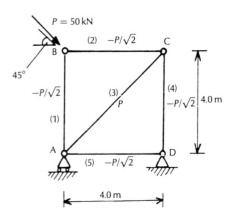

Truss geometry and member forces

material strength. The value of the buckling stress depends primarily on the length of the member and on its stiffness (moment of inertia).

There is only one design parameter for an axially acting member with a given cross-section shape – the area of the cross-section.

6.3.4.1 Tension members

There is only one member in tension – member 3. The member force is:

$$N_t = P = 50\,\text{kN}$$

Adopting a safety factor of 2.0 against yielding of the member, the required cross-section area is obtained from:

$$\sigma_t = N_t/A \le 230/2.0 = 115\,\text{N/mm}^2$$
$$\Rightarrow A_{req} \ge N_t/115 = 50\,000/115 = 435\,\text{mm}^2$$

A tube of 76 mm outside diameter and 2.0 mm wall thickness fits the bill.

6.3.4.2 Compression members

All remaining members are compression members with a compression force of:

$$N_c = P/\sqrt{2} = 50\,000/\sqrt{2} = 35\,355\,\text{N}$$

The detailed treatment of buckling is quite involved, but for a large range of practical cases the length–stiffness configuration is such that the permissible compressive stress is approximately $\frac{1}{3}$ of the permissible tensile stress (for tubular members this corresponds approximately to diameters of $\frac{1}{25}$–$\frac{1}{50}$ of the length). Using this value as a rough guideline, the required cross-section area is obtained as:

$$A_{req} \ge 3 \times N_c/115 = 3 \times 35\,355/115 = 922\,\text{mm}^2$$

A tube of 89 mm outside diameter and 3.65 mm wall thickness has a cross-section area of 979 mm². The actual capacity of this tube when buckling

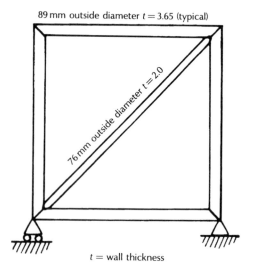

89 mm outside diameter $t = 3.65$ (typical)

76 mm outside diameter $t = 2.0$

t = wall thickness

Truss member design

and code requirements are taken into account is approximately 90 kN (based on load tables in the literature). The compression force of 35 kN, therefore, represents a somewhat conservative design for the safe load (providing a safety factor of 2.6).

Part II Characteristics of Structural Systems

7 Stability, Rigidity and Classification of Structures

7.1 Introduction

Stability and *Rigidity* are basic concepts. How-ever, they relate to a structural system as a whole and not just to parts of structures (such as members), and so a discussion of these concepts serves as a transition to the second part of the book, which is concerned with structural systems. There is a lack of consistency in the technical literature with regard to these concepts, and the meaning sometimes depends on the context or on the background of the practitioners. Other terms are sometimes employed to indicate the same thing. The definitions that follow are intuitively clear. They are general and, at the same time, rigorous enough to characterise properly the desired properties of structural systems.

7.2 Stability

Stability is the ability of a structure to support load while undergoing **limited** deformations and displacements. The limit of deformation or dis-placement which determines if a structure is stable or not depends on the type of structure (see *Rigidity* below).

Stability is a **qualitative** term – a structure is stable or unstable. It cannot be 'more stable' or 'less stable'. Two kinds of stability are distin-guished – geometric and elastic – depending on the source of instability, if it occurs.

7.2.1 Geometric stability

Geometric stability is the ability of a structure to support any load at all. This is a property of the **geometry** of the structure (hence the term). It is not related to the magnitude of the load or

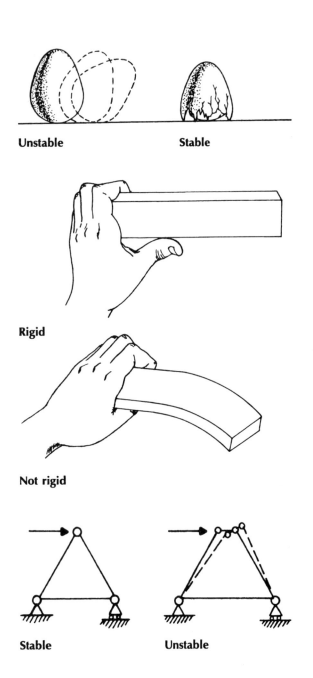

Unstable   **Stable**

Rigid

Not rigid

Stable   **Unstable**

the strength of the components of the structure. It is sometimes termed **general stability** or **overall stability**. Unless noted otherwise, the term 'stability' implies 'geometric stability' in this book.

7.2.2 Elastic stability – buckling

Elastic stability or *Buckling* is a mode of **structural failure**. It is a function of the load and of the stiffness of the structure and its components. Buckling is characteristic of structures or parts of structures in compression. Buckling is a phenomenon of **loss of stability** in geometrically stable structures, when the load reaches a certain 'critical' value – the *Buckling load*. As mentioned, buckling is a mode of failure and it should not be confused with normal modes of action such as bending or axial action.

7.2.3 Types of buckling

7.2.3.1 General buckling
This can relate to isolated members or to whole structures. Members in axial compression, such as columns or truss members in compression, are subject to general buckling (see 8.1). Structures which act primarily in compression, such as *arches*, *domes* and *shells* (Chapters 9 and 11), are also subject to this mode of failure.

7.2.3.2 Lateral buckling
This is characteristic of the compressed parts of beams (the parts in tension tend to remain straight). As a result, the beam tends to twist (this mode of failure is also termed 'lateral torsional buckling').

7.2.3.3 Local buckling
This is characteristic of compressed regions of structures or structural components having small thickness, for example cold-formed sections (6.2.1) and thin shells. As the term implies, buckling occurs in specific locations in the member or structure. Nevertheless, this mode of failure often

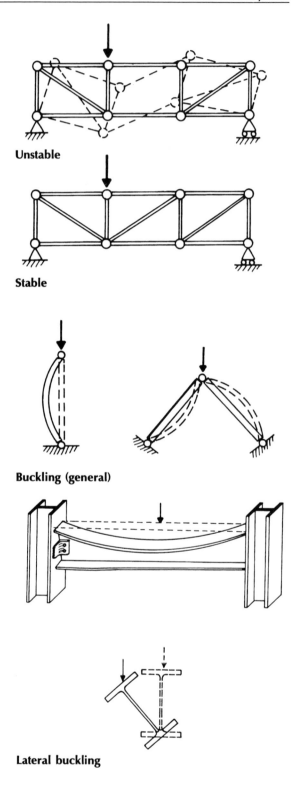

Unstable

Stable

Buckling (general)

Lateral buckling

represents the mode of failure of the structure as a whole due to the brittle failure mode which often characterises buckling (6.1.5).

7.3 Rigidity and deformability

The concept of rigidity is related, both semantically and thematically, to the concept of **stiffness**, introduced in Chapter 5. Rigidity is a property of the geometry of the structure alone, and does not depend on the size of its components or on the structural depth. Stiffness or *Elastic stiffness*, to be precise, is an expression of relation between force and displacement. Both concepts are related to **motion**. **Elasticity** is a **quantitative** parameter, it is related to the **amount** of motion under increasing load. *Rigidity* or, more precisely, *Geometric rigidity* is a **qualitative** term indicating the **absence** of motion under 'vanishingly small' loads. While a structure can be stiff to a higher or lesser degree, it is either rigid or it is *deformable*.

Deformability or, more precisely, *Geometric deformability* is the property of a structure whereby the structure changes its shape under a load, however small. It is the inverse of rigidity, much like 'flexibility' is the inverse term of 'stiffness'. However, while a structure generally possesses both flexibility and stiffness, a structure is **either rigid or deformable**. In this book, the terms 'rigidity' and 'deformability' are synonymous with 'geometric rigidity' and 'geometric deformability'.

7.3.1 Rigid and deformable structures

Rigid structures and deformable structures are two distinct types of structures. A rigid structure is capable of sustaining the applied loads without noticeable changes to its shape (geometry). Beams and trusses, encountered in Chapter 4, are examples of rigid structures.

Deformable structures, on the other hand, cannot support load in their original geometry. They change their shape to fit the applied load.

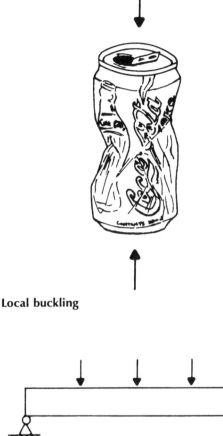

Local buckling

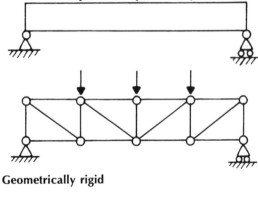

Geometrically rigid

Geometrically deformable

However, the deformations involved are still within the 'limited' range (7.2), allowing this type of structure to be considered 'stable'.

The simplest example of a deformable structure is a cable stretched between two points (a clothes line, for instance). Fabric structures are another example (e.g. tents).

7.4 Comments on stability and rigidity

Stability and rigidity are both qualitative terms but they are distinct concepts. A structure can be deformable and stable at the same time (although, by definition, it may not be geometrically rigid and unstable at the same time).

An unstable structure is not acceptable (since it cannot support load). A structure can, however, undergo temporary stages of instability. For instance, *Deployable structures* are structures designed deliberately as unstable during the erection process. In the erected position, however, they must be stabilised (e.g. an umbrella). An unstable structure is a *Mechanism*.

> Some of the confusion in terminology in the technical literature stems from the failure to distinguish between the concepts of stability and rigidity. It is not uncommon to find in the literature deformable structures termed 'unstable'. In other sources they appear under a variety of terms (e.g. 'kinematically indeterminate'), but the term 'deformable' or 'geometrically deformable' is more intuitive.

7.5 Pin-jointed frameworks

The definitions of statical determinacy and stability (5.1, 7.2) imply that a statically determinate structure is 'just stable' – it is capable of providing exactly the number of internal and reaction force components required to balance the applied loads. Removal of one member or one restraint (at the supports) will render the structure unstable. Obviously, a statically redundant structure is stable.

Stable, deformable

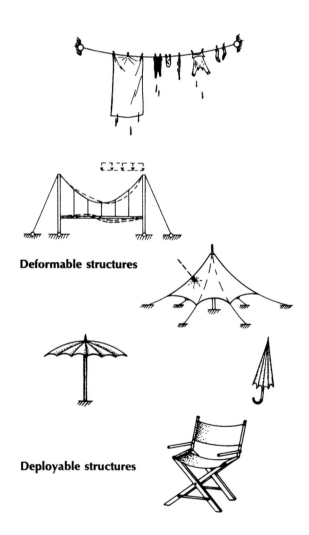

Deformable structures

Deployable structures

7.5.1 Statical conditions

The condition for stability of a **rigid** bar structure is that there are at least enough internal member force and reaction components to satisfy equilibrium.

It has been observed (4.8.5) that the available number of equilibrium equations in a planar truss is twice the number of joints. If we denote by m the number of members, by j the number of joints and by r the number of restraints (that is of reaction force components) then the requirement for **stability** of planar trusses (or any pin-jointed planar structure) is:

$$m + r \geq 2j$$

7.5.1.1 A distinction should be made between a (geometrically) *Rigid structure* and a *Rigid body*. An unrestrained body is a rigid body, if it maintains its shape (though not its position) under load. The minimum number of reaction components needed to stabilise a rigid body in the plane is three (restraining two translation directions and rotation). If the structure, without the reactions, is not a rigid body it will need more reaction components to stabilise it. Setting $r = 3$ in the above equation yields a condition for the number of members required to make the truss a rigid body.

$$m \geq 2j - 3$$

7.5.1.2 Rigid jointed bar structures are automatically geometrically rigid bodies, and they are stable if they maintain overall equilibrium, that is they have at least three independent reaction components in the plane (see conditions for independence below). In following discussions, when reference is made to a bar structure as 'rigid', a 'rigid body' is implied (deformable bar structures are a rarity).

In spatial trusses – three-dimensional pin-jointed structures – the number of equilibrium equations at each joint is three, and the minimum number of

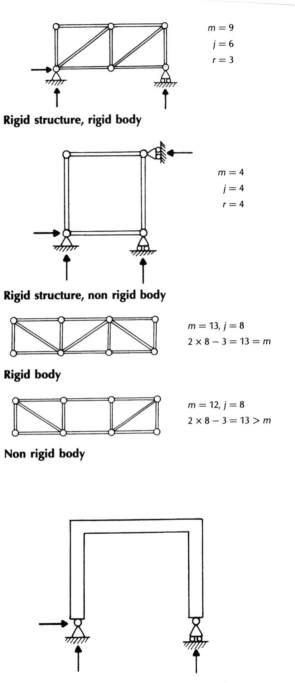

$m = 9$
$j = 6$
$r = 3$

Rigid structure, rigid body

$m = 4$
$j = 4$
$r = 4$

Rigid structure, non rigid body

$m = 13, j = 8$
$2 \times 8 - 3 = 13 = m$

Rigid body

$m = 12, j = 8$
$2 \times 8 - 3 = 13 > m$

Non rigid body

Rigid-jointed structure (geometrically rigid)

reaction components is six. Therefore the equations above can be extended for use with space trusses as well, with the substitution of $3j$ instead of $2j$, and $r = 6$ instead of $r = 3$.

7.5.1.3 Unfortunately, **the conditions for stability and rigidity detailed above are insufficient**. A structure can satisfy them while not being stable and/or rigid. It is not enough for a structure to possess the necessary number of members and restraints, but these members and restraints have to be appropriately located and oriented.

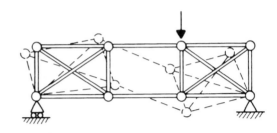

$m = 14, j = 8, r = 3; m + r = 17 > 2 \times 8$
but unstable

7.5.2 General rules

The following three rules are sufficient in most cases to assess the rigidity and stability of planar pin-jointed networks. Unfortunately their direct application is practical only for relatively simple geometries.

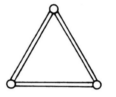

Geometrically rigid (body) (1)

Rigid connection of joint (2)

7.5.2.1 Rule 1
A triangle is a rigid pin-jointed polygon (the only one).

7.5.2.2 Rule 2
A joint connected to a rigid body/structure by two non parallel bars is rigid, i.e. the structure consisting of the original structure + the two new bars is also rigid.

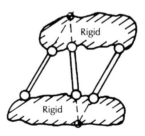

Rigid connection of two rigid bodies (3)

7.5.2.3 Rule 3
A structure/body consisting of two rigid parts connected by three bars that do not all intersect at a common point is rigid. Parallel bars are considered to be intersecting (at infinity).

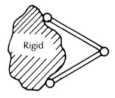

Rigid body

Rigid body

7.5.2.4 Comments
(1) The ground is considered a rigid body. The requirement for stability is thus a requirement that the structure forms a rigid body with the ground.

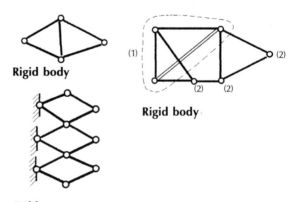

Stable

(2) The rules above do not apply to deformable structures, but rule 3 applies to the directions of reaction components to ensure overall stability of both rigid and deformable structures. It ensures the 'independence' of reaction components.

The three rules above are in fact one fundamental rule which makes a connection between rigidity and graphic rules. Essentially, a pin-jointed structure is rigid if it can be drawn uniquely by using a protractor and ruler (tape measure). This is due to the correspondence of a pin-jointed member with the direction of the force in it.

There are mathematical procedures for the testing of rigidity and stability. They fall in the area of linear algebra, but their application requires the use of computers. With few exceptions (see below), there are no simple ways to ascertain the rigidity and stability of complex networks.

A method for the testing of the rigidity of a quadrilateral planar grid

A rectangular grid, or any planar grid formed of four-sided (quadrilateral) cells, is not a rigid body, as can be confirmed by applying the formula in 7.5.1. In order to rigidify the network, it is necessary to introduce diagonals in some of the cells. The questions are: (1) How many? (2) Where?

It is easy to verify, using the above rules, that introducing diagonals in all the cells along two adjacent boundaries is sufficient to rigidify the network as a whole. It turns out that this is also the smallest number of diagonals required for the purpose (7.5.1). However, it is by no means the only way to do it.

To check if a given diagonalised network is rigid, assuming the number of diagonals is sufficient, do the following:

❑ Identify each cell of the network by a letter and a number, representing the corresponding column and row (similar to the location of squares in a city map).

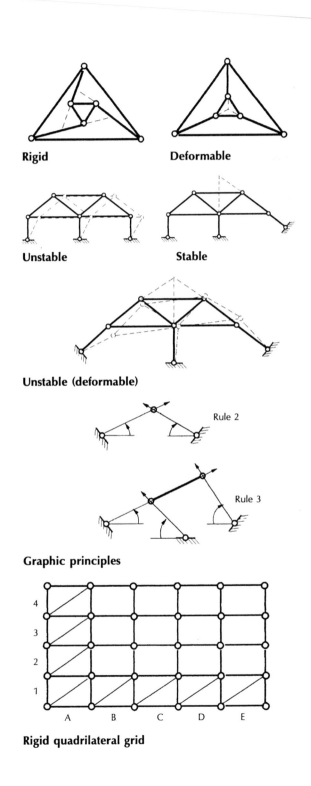

Rigid   **Deformable**

Unstable   **Stable**

Unstable (deformable)

Rule 2

Rule 3

Graphic principles

Rigid quadrilateral grid

- ❑ Draw two parallel lines of dots. The dots in one line are identified by the cell letters (say, of columns), the other line contains the cell numbers (say rows).
- ❑ Connect a dot from one row with a dot in the other, if the cell identified by the letter and number contains a diagonal. The resulting drawing is called a 'bipartite graph' in graph theory.
- ❑ The grid is rigid if the bipartite graph is **connected**, i.e. if it is possible to 'travel' from any dot to any other dot in the graph through some combination of lines. Otherwise, the grid is not rigid.

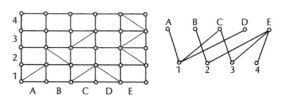

Rigid

7.6 A classification scheme for structural systems

Structures, like any other group of objects, can be classified in many different ways. (We have already encountered planar and spatial, rigid and deformable structures etc.) The purpose of a classification scheme is to highlight major features common to items in any category of the scheme, and therefore it depends on the main context or theme under which the objects are compared.

The main theme of the present work is the relation between the shape or geometry of a structure and the way in which it supports the applied loads, namely the mode of **action** of its components (3.7.4).

Accordingly, the scheme adopted in the following chapters consists of a matrix whose rows represent geometries and whose columns represent modes of action.

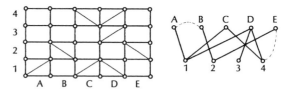

Not rigid

7.6.1 Geometry

7.6.1.1 We have encountered one major geometrical class – bar structures. From the geometrical viewpoint they can be termed *Discrete structures*. Most of their surface or volume is void and material is confined to elongated members. If the

Geometry	Action mode		
	Direct		**Flexure**
Discrete, reticulated, bar structures	Planar	Rigid Deformable	Planar
	Spatial	Rigid Deformable	Spatial
Continuous (solid) structures	Planar	Rigid	Planar
	Spatial	Deformable	Spatial

structure consists of a mesh of slender members it is sometimes termed a **Reticulated structure** or **Lattice structure**. A truss is a typical example. Reticulated structures are typically constructed of steel members.

7.6.1.2 The other major class of structures from the geometrical viewpoint is **Continuous structures** or **Solid structures**. These are structures whose surface or volume is taken up mostly by matter (and not by voids). The isolated beam can be considered a continuous structure, although in the analytical process we considered it a single bar.

7.6.1.3 If we consider a system of intersecting beams we get a discrete structure called a **Beam grid**. If we fill in the voids in the grid of beams, we obtain a continuous structure called a **Slab**. (We can obtain it equivalently by starting with a beam and increasing its width.) Continuous structures are typically constructed of reinforced concrete.

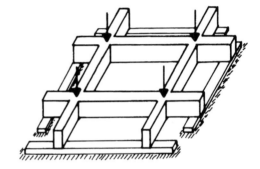

Beam grid

7.6.2 Mode of action

We have already encountered the two major modes of action.

7.6.2.1 The truss acts through axial forces only (compression or tension). This mode of action is termed **Direct action**. This concept is further expanded to other than bar structures in Chapter 10, but the main point is that **in direct action the structural depth of the structure exceeds by far the depth of the individual member or component.** The stabilising moment is obtained as a couple formed by the forces in different members, or by member forces and reaction forces.

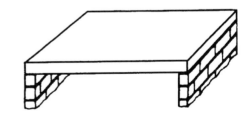

Slab

7.6.2.2 The beam or slab, on the other hand, acts in **Flexure**. It is subject to shear force and bending moment (and may also be subjected to axial force). The main point, however, is that **in flexure, structural depth is confined within the depth of the member**. The stabilising moment is primarily the bending moment.

There are structures which combine flexure and direct action, and some such structures are encountered in subsequent chapters.

Geometry	Action mode	
	Direct	**Flexure**
Discrete	**Truss**	**Beam grid**
Continuous	**Column**	**Beam** **Slab**

8 Planar Bar Structures

This and the following chapters look at some common structural systems and highlight the main topics in the design and behaviour of these systems. Chapter 8 deals with planar structures consisting of essentially straight members, starting with a single bar in different modes of action and proceeding in increasing degree of complexity to multi-bar systems.

8.1 Bar in compression

The most common failure mode of compressed bars is by buckling (7.2.2). If the axial force is gradually increased it reaches a limiting value – P_{cr} – when the bar starts bending significantly. So long as the bar remains elastic (6.1.1) the force remains at its critical value as the bar continues bending. Upon release of the load, the bar straightens.

8.1.1 Parameter affecting bar buckling

It is straightforward to formulate an intuitive expression for the parameters affecting the value of the buckling force:

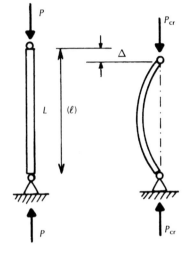

Column buckling

$$P_{cr} = \text{Const} \times \frac{(\text{Material stiffness}) \times (x - \text{section dimensions})}{\text{Member length}}$$

$$P_{cr} = \text{Const} \, \frac{E \times I}{\ell^2}$$

It was seen in Chapter 5 that the parameter expressing material stiffness is the modulus of elasticity, E, and the parameter expressing cross-section dimension (spread of material) is the moment of inertia, I. The power 2 for the length is required for consistency of units: P_{cr} is in N; E is in N/mm^2; I is in mm^4 and ℓ is in mm.

8.1.1.1 The actual expression for what is known as Euler's buckling force (Leonard Euler, 1707–1783) is:

$$P_{cr} = \pi^2 \frac{EI}{\ell^2}$$

This is a theoretical expression. It gives, for the buckling (or 'critical') stress, the expression:

$$\sigma_{cr} = \frac{\pi^2 E}{\ell^2 (A/I)} = \frac{\pi^2 E}{(\ell/i)^2}; \qquad i = \sqrt{\frac{I}{A}}$$

The parameter 'i' is termed the **Radius of gyration** and it has units of length. The ratio ℓ/i is termed the **Slenderness ratio** and it is dimensionless.

As the slenderness ratio decreases, Euler's buckling stress increases, tending to infinity as the slenderness ratio vanishes. This is clearly nonsense, since the upper limit of the buckling stress is the yield strength of the material. Euler's formula applies only to elastic buckling, where the stress remains below the yield point.

In practice, the buckling load is always lower than the theoretical Euler value, due to imperfections such as lack of straightness of the member. The deviation from Euler's load is largest in the region of slenderness ratios where Euler's buckling load approaches the yield strength – the 'transition' slenderness ratio (for mild steel this slenderness ratio is approximately 80). Columns which possess a substantially lower slenderness ratio than the transitional are termed 'stub columns' and they fail by yielding rather than by buckling. It turns out that, in practice, the majority of axially compressed steel members fall in the zone of slenderness ratios close to the transition value: 70–140. In this range buckling is a brittle type of failure (6.1.5) and therefore conducive to *progressive collapse* (10.7.1.3). The actual buckling stress near the transitional slenderness ratio, according to codes, is approximately 0.6–0.7 Euler's buckling load. (It varies somewhat with type and size of the cross-section and with different codes).

For thin-walled tubes $i = r/\sqrt{2}$ (r is the mean radius of the tube), so slenderness ratios in the

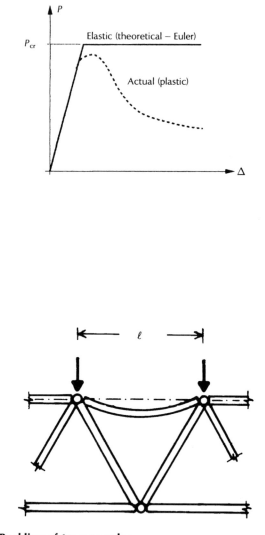

Buckling of truss member

range mentioned above translate into a diameter range of $\ell/25-\ell/50$ (see 6.3.4.2).

8.1.1.2 The length ℓ is the **Buckling length**, which depends on the end conditions of the bar. For a pin-ended bar it is equal to the actual length of the bar. For a fixed-ended bar, the buckling length is half the bar length.

In general, the buckling length can be inferred from the (intuitive) shape of the buckled member. The buckling length is the distance along the member's axis between **Inflexion points** – the points where the curvature changes sense. A hinge is an inflexion point. An inflexion point may lie outside the member ends, particularly when one of the ends is free to move laterally. (The inflexion points are obtained by 'extending' the member with respect to the fixed end.)

8.2 Single bar in tension

A bar which acts in axial tension, and is not liable to be in compression under some loading conditions, is very efficient in utilising its strength, since it does not require flexural stiffness. Such a bar, often termed a **Tie**, typically has a small cross-section compared with a bar in compression of equal magnitude. Ties sometimes take the form of a **Cable** – a member of multi-stranded cross-section having negligible flexural stiffness. The term 'cable' refers also to a curved member having the *funicular shape* (9.1).

If a tension force is somehow introduced to a tie before it is loaded, so that it is initially in tension, then it can resist compressive load, even when it has small flexural stiffness, so long as the net force in the bar remains tensile.

8.3 Prestress

A state in which internal forces exist in a structure with no load being applied is termed a state of

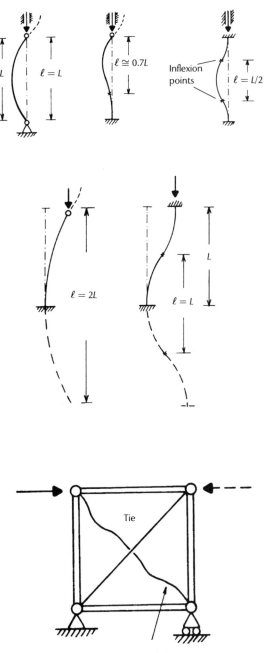

Tie slackens under load from left, tightens when load is reversed

Prestress. A tensile prestress is sometimes referred to as ***Pretension.***

A straight, pretensioned bar is a ***Tendon.*** The terms 'tendon' and 'cable' are often used interchangeably, because tendons are often made of cables (8.2).

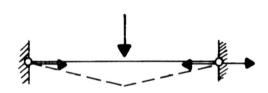

Prestressed tendon

8.3.1 *Prestressable structures*

Not all structures can be prestressed. The simplest way to see if a pin-jointed bar structure is prestressable is to 'cut' one of the bars and introduce tension in it by 'pulling' on the cut ends. If this operation introduces forces into the remaining members, the structure is prestressable. In the case of geometrically rigid structures, this will happen if the structure with the 'cut' member removed is stable.

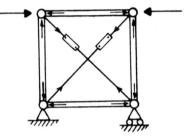

Prestressed tendons. Both are active under any load

8.3.1.1 It follows immediately that **statically indeterminate structures are prestressable** (at least in part), since they have redundancy of internal forces (or reactions), and therefore it is possible to remove a member and still maintain equilibrium.

8.3.1.2 It is equally apparent that **a statically determinate structure is not prestressable**, since it has no members to spare. 'Pulling' the cut member simply changes the shape of the structure but does not introduce forces into other members.

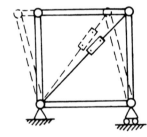

Statically determinate truss is not prestressable

8.3.1.3 It is less obvious that a **geometrically deformable structure is prestressable**. Indeed, prestress is often a requirement in order to keep deflections within acceptable limits. By looking at the equilibrium of a simple tendon 'stretched' between two fixed joints it can be verified that the deflection is inversely proportional (though not linearly) to the **pretension** force.

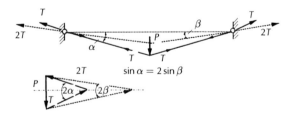

8.3.2 *Prestressability and environmental effects*

The property of prestressability has implications for the sensitivity of structures to **environmental effects** (2.1.3), such as temperature variations and support settlement.

Statically indeterminate structures are sensitive to these effects because the change in length of a member (due to temperature change) introduces forces in other members. A support movement may also introduce internal forces, if the static indeterminacy involves redundancy of reactions.

Statically determinate structures undergo geometrical changes but no forces are introduced. For this reason structures in sensitive environments (such as loose soils), or exposed structures, are sometimes deliberately designed as statically determinate by the introduction of adequate releases to allow motion, for example expansion joints in bridges.

Geometrically deformable structures are not usually sensitive to environmental effects in spite of their prestressability. The magnitude of environmentally induced motions is usually small compared with the deformations caused by the applied load and therefore the induced forces are correspondingly small.

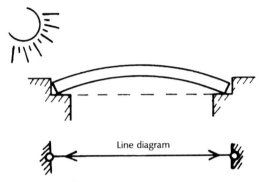

Buckling due to thermal expansion

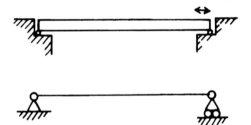

Statically determinate – no thermal stresses

8.4 Bar in bending – beam

In Chapter 4 the statically determinate configurations of simply supported and cantilever beams were analysed in some detail. We saw there the relation between load, moment diagrams and deflected shape. These rules apply, in general, also to more complex configurations such as statically indeterminate beams.

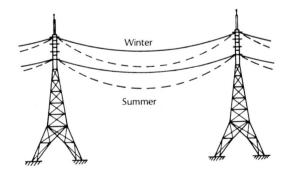

8.4.1 *Summary of flexural features*

❑ The shape of the moment diagram is a function of the nature of the load.
❑ The moment diagram of uniformly distributed load is a parabola (of second degree).
❑ The value of the moment at mid span of a simply supported beam is $qL^2/8$ (q is the intensity of the distributed load and L is the span).
❑ The moment diagram along segments with no loads is a straight line. It follows that for a load consisting of a series of concentrated loads, the moment diagram is polygonal. (Demonstrate it by analysing a cantilever with a point load at the end. Refer to 4.3.)
❑ The relation between the bending moment (internal couple) and deflected shape results from the fact that the tensioned face of the beam elongates and becomes convex, while the compressed side shortens and becomes concave.

When the bending moment is drawn as a curved arrow the arrow points into the compressed/concave face.

❑ When following the convention of drawing the moment diagram on the tensioned face the relation between the direction of the load (distributed or concentrated) and the curvature of the diagram is like the tip of an umbrella's rod to its hood (or to the shape of a cable under the same load, see Chapter 9).
❑ The *Arrow* of the parabola of the moment diagram of a uniformly distributed load for any span, or any segment of length L, is $qL^2/8$. The arrow is the maximum vertical distance (perpendicular to the member) between the parabola and its chord. This maximum occurs at mid length of the chord (at $L/2$).

Following are some examples of common statically indeterminate beams.

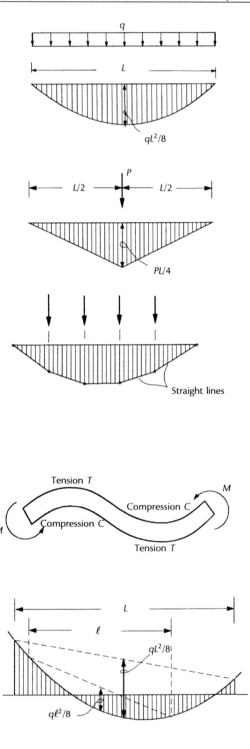

8.4.2 Propped cantilever

A propped cantilever (5.1.1.2, 5.4) is a cantilever whose end is supported by a roller. It is simple to draw the moment diagram qualitatively (given the moment at the roller is zero) for any load, based on the intuitive deflected shape.

With the additional information that the moment at the fixed end for a uniformly distributed load is $qL^2/8$ (tension on top) it is possible to compute the moment and shear force at any cross-section (using free-body diagrams). This value applies provided the cross-section does not change along the span – the member is a **Prismatic member.**

8.4.3 Fixed-ended beam

A **Fixed-ended beam** is a beam with both ends fixed. In this case there are moments at both ends of the beam. For symmetric loads (such as a uniformly distributed load or concentrated load at the centre), these two moments are equal and the moment at mid span is equal to the moment for the simply supported beam less the fixed-end moment. For a prismatic member loaded with a uniformly distributed load, the fixed-end moment is $qL^2/12$.

8.5 Continuous beam

A **Continuous beam** consists of a number of beams joined rigidly end to end, over several supports. One of the supports is hinged, the remaining are rollers, for analytical purposes. Since the connection of the supports to the beam is hinged, the supports cannot be subject to moment, so there are two reaction components at the hinged support and one (vertical) reaction at each roller. In the beam itself, however, there is a bending moment (internal couple) over the support due to the continuity of the members.

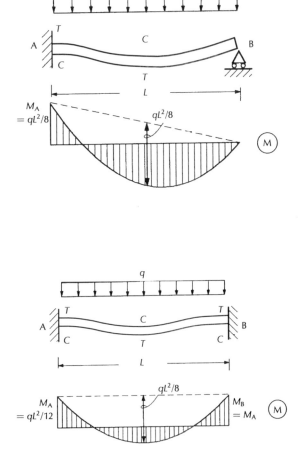

Looking at the deflected shape, the moment diagram under a uniformly distributed load is seen to be a series of parabolas changing sides in accordance with the changing sense of the curvature. The sharp cusp in the moment diagram over the supports is due to the concentrated reaction force.

The magnitudes of the **Support moments** depend on the relative span lengths, the values of the loads on each span and the cross-sections (moments of inertia) of each span. Values for regular configurations can be found in tables in the technical literature. In a beam of regular spans (approximately equal) loaded with a uniform loading, the support moments can be approximated as $qL^2/10$ for the first interior support from each end, and $qL^2/12$ for other interior supports.

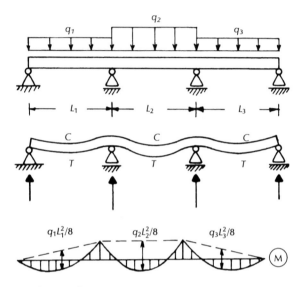

Continuous beam

8.6 Some design considerations for beams

8.6.1 Depth/span ratios

It was shown in 6.3.2 that the depth of a simply supported steel beam, when strength and deflection are considered, is usually of the order of $\frac{1}{20}$ of the span. In 6.3.3 the rule of thumb for the depth of a concrete beam was given as $\frac{1}{10}$ of the span.

These figures can be extended to other types of beams and frames, provided that the span is substituted with an 'equivalent span'. The equivalent span is the span of a simply supported beam that would produce the same maximum deflection. The following table provides the equivalent span, L_{eq}, as a portion of the actual span, L:

$$L_{eq} = C \times L$$

Span type	C
Simply supported	1.0
Fixed-hinged (propped cantilever or external span of continuous beams)	0.8
Fixed-fixed (fixed-ended beam or interior spans of continuous beams)	0.6
Cantilever beam	2.2

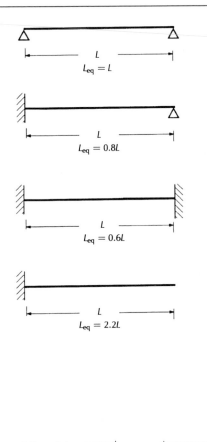

The values for continuous beams apply to beams in which the spans do not vary considerably in length and load, and the load on each span is uniformly distributed.

When the beam supports a concrete slab, the slab thickness is included in the beam depth for concrete beams. It is also included in the depth of a steel beam if the beam is built compositely with the slab – see slab systems below (8.8).

8.6.2 Lateral buckling

It should be remembered (7.2.3.2) that the compressed fibres in a beam are subject to lateral buckling as a mode of failure, unless lateral buckling is prevented. Steel beams, in particular, are subject to this form of failure. Lateral bracing should be provided to the compressed flanges of steel beams. If the flange is attached to a slab or roof system (8.8, 8.11), restraint is provided to that flange. It should be noted that in a cantilever beam the compressed flange is at the bottom (and may not be attached to a slab), and in a continuous beam or propped cantilever or fixed-ended beam, the compressed flange is at the top at mid span and at the bottom near interior supports or fixed ends. If a compressed flange is not attached to other structural elements, special restraints have to be provided at regular intervals.

Concrete beams are not usually susceptible to lateral buckling due to their relatively large width.

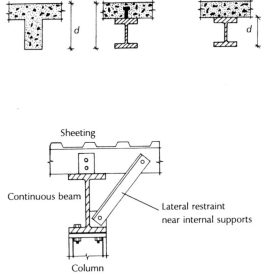

Lateral restraint of roof beam

8.7 One-way slab

We have defined a slab (7.6.1.3) as a structure
having essentially a planar geometry with two
dimensions (length and width) considerably larger
than the third (thickness) and subject to bending
action, namely loaded perpendicular to its surface. Slabs are normally constructed of reinforced
concrete.

If the slab has roughly rectangular layout and is
supported along two opposite edges, or if it is
supported along all four edges but the length of
the rectangular plan is considerably larger than
the width, then it acts as a very wide beam
spanning between the parallel supports, or across
the width. We can 'cut' a narrow strip of unit
width (say 1 m) parallel to the spanning direction
and consider this strip as a beam, representative
of the slab, all strips being essentially identical.
Such a slab is termed a *One-way slab*.

Although from the geometrical viewpoint a slab
is a continuous structure, a one-way slab is
considered a beam from the analytical viewpoint,
and therefore a bar structure. The slab may be
continuous over several spans, in which case it is
analysed as a continuous beam.

If a slab has a roughly square layout and is supported along all four boundaries, it spans in two,
mutually perpendicular directions. This is a *two-
way slab*, which is essentially a spatial structure
and it is considered in Chapter 10.

When the width and length dimensions of the plan
of a slab supported on all four edges are similar –
length $\leq$ ~1.5 × width – then any point close to
the centre of the slab is supported by the slab
spanning in both directions. This is because the
point would deflect a similar amount if it was supported in either direction alone.

If, on the other hand, the length is considerably
greater than the width, then the deflection of
the point near the centre of the slab is governed
by the short span – the span across the width –
since this deflection is considerably smaller than

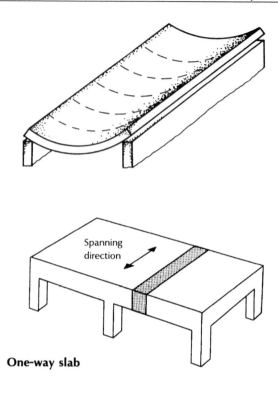

One-way slab

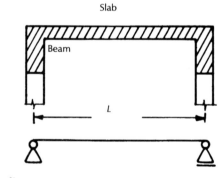

Line diagram

would be obtained across the larger span. The effect of the side supports is felt only in the close vicinity of these edges, but interior points behave as though they were supported along the long edges only.

In general, when several load paths are available (in two directions, in this case), the load will be distributed among these paths in direct proportion to their relative stiffness.

8.7.1 Ribbed slab

A **Ribbed slab** is a form of 'dilution' of the one-way slab. In order to increase structural depth of concrete slabs without increase in weight, the slab is converted into a series of beams – 'ribs' – at close spacing, with a thin layer of concrete joining them. The spacing between the ribs is formed by lightweight infill bodies, such as lightweight blocks, cardboard or foamed polymer boxes etc.

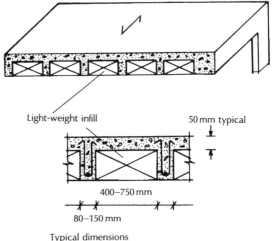

Light-weight infill   50 mm typical
400–750 mm
80–150 mm
Typical dimensions

Ribbed slab

8.8 Planar one-way slab systems

A slab, which is normally of reinforced concrete, is usually supported on a framework of beams and columns or *frames*. The supporting framework may be made of steel or concrete members.

8.8.1 Steel framed slab systems

A typical steel framed slab system usually consists of the following components:

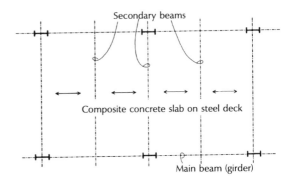

Secondary beams
Composite concrete slab on steel deck
Main beam (girder)

- The slab is often cast on a **Steel deck**. The deck serves both as formwork and as bottom reinforcement to the slab, with which it acts compositely (6.2.2.1). The composite action of such a **Composite slab** is facilitated by the bond between the deck and the concrete.
- The slab is supported directly on a system of **Secondary beams**. These beams also often act compositely with the slab as **Composite beams**, by means of **Shear connectors**. The slab acts as

the compression flange of the beam. The shear connectors transfer the horizontal shear force between the slab and the beam (see 5.7.1.3).

- The secondary beams are supported on the main beams called *Girders* which, in turn, are supported on the columns. The girders also often act compositely with the slab.

This is a highly efficient structural system because the steel and concrete components act compositely – steel in tension, concrete in compression. The concrete slab prevents lateral buckling of the steel beams and girders.

8.8.2 Concrete framed slab systems

8.8.2.1 The basic support hierarchy of slab–secondary beams–girders applies also to concrete slab of systems. The slab may be cast on site monolithically (together) with the beams. This is a labour intensive and often uneconomical method, particularly for large buildings, because it involves extensive and expensive site labour such as formwork manufacturing and erection, and laying of reinforcement. Industrialised techniques involve the use of *Precast concrete* components such as precast beams and slab units. These are prefabricated concrete elements produced in specialised plants. This method reduces labour and speeds erection. Precast slab units can also be used in conjunction with steel framed systems.

8.8.2.2 The components of precast concrete slab systems and other prefabricated concrete structures (bridges, for example) are often in the form of *Prestressed concrete*. In this technique, compression is introduced into the concrete cross-section by means of tensioned steel tendons (8.3). Since the concrete is initially in compression, it is capable of sustaining tensile stress in the same way that a tensioned tendon can sustain compressive force. Prestressed concrete sections are

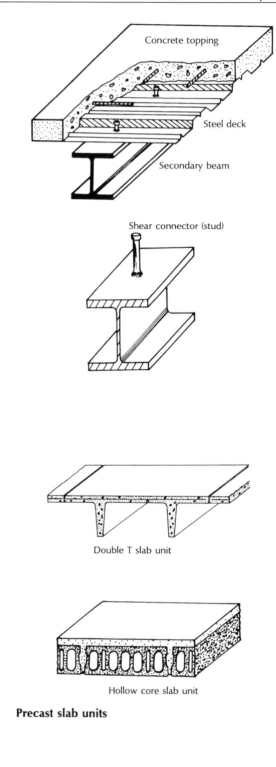

Precast slab units

usually designed so that no net tensile stress arises in the cross-section and therefore the section is uncracked. The effective cross-section for strength and deflection computation is, therefore, the full cross-section.

Sometimes sections are designed as **partially prestressed**, chiefly for economic reasons. Such partially prestressed sections do undergo a limited amount of cracking.

The prestressing technique usually employed in prestressed, precast concrete components is called **pretensioning**. The tendons are tensioned against a steel frame prior to casting the element within the frame. After hardening of the concrete, the tendons are cut from the frame and compression is transferred to the concrete through the bond between the tendons and the concrete. A different technique, which is suitable also for cast-in-place elements, is **post-tensioning**. The prestressing tendons are inserted in ducts which are cast in the concrete element. After hardening of the concrete, the tendons are tensioned against specially designed end anchors embedded in the concrete.

8.8.3 Depth/span ratios for slabs

As for beams, 'rules of thumb' can be formulated for estimating slab thickness, based primarily on deflection requirements. For a one-way solid slab this value is of the order of $\frac{1}{30}-\frac{1}{25}$ of the equivalent span. For ribbed slabs it is in the range $\frac{1}{25}-\frac{1}{20}$ of the equivalent span.

In steel framed slab systems the values are: deck–slab: $\frac{1}{30}$ of the equivalent spans between secondary beams (total thickness); secondary beams: approximately $\frac{1}{25}-\frac{1}{20}$ of the beam span, including the thickness of the slab; girders: $\frac{1}{20}-\frac{1}{15}$ of the girder span (including the slab).

Composite beams and girders are usually designed as simply supported, in order to avoid compression in the bottom, unrestrained flange.

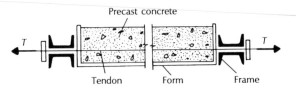

Pretensioned prestressed concrete element

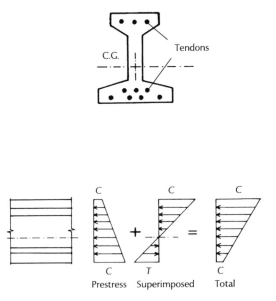

Stress distribution in cross-section of prestressed beam

Composite deck slabs are also often designed as simply supported (and hence equivalent span equals actual span), but continuity can be obtained through addition of top reinforcement over the supporting beams (where the top fibre is in tension).

Depth/span ratios for prestressed concrete components are generally 25–30% lower than the corresponding non prestressed values, due to the increased effective stiffness of the cross-section.

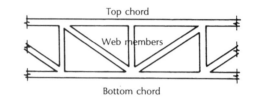

Dilution of beam − truss

8.9 Dilution of material − *Discretisation*

It is always possible to 'transform' a continuous structure into an 'equivalent' discrete or reticulated structure, through the process of material dilution. The bulk of the material is removed from zones where it does not contribute much to strength and stiffness and concentrated in discrete members. Typically there are many ways of diluting of a continuous system, providing a range of geometries and modes of action.

8.9.1 *Discretisation of the beam − truss*

One way of 'diluting a beam' is to 'cut' triangular holes out of it, leaving two bunches of fibres adjacent to the main tension and compression faces − the **Chords** − and a system of short bars − the **Web members** or **Webs** − forming with the chords a triangular network. Dilution of a beam into a truss not only transforms it from continuous to discrete, but also from flexure to direct action.

The web members ensure the cooperation of the chords and the resistance to shear forces. There are many possible configurations of chord and web layouts, which are equivalent to a given beam. Structural efficiency can be improved by varying structural depth in accordance with the moment diagram of the beam. For instance, a simply supported truss can have its structural depth increased in the centre of the span by giving it a triangular or trapezoidal shape.

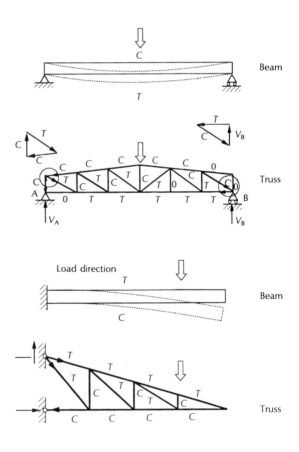

The types of forces in the members of the resulting truss (tension compression) can be derived by analogy with the beam. Typically, the forces in the chords are similar to the forces in the corresponding fibres of the beam. For instance, the top chord of a simply supported truss is in compression and the bottom chord is in tension.

The forces in web members are less obvious. In a simply supported configuration it is best to look near a support and derive (from equilibrium) the force in the nearest diagonal member. The forces in adjacent diagonals typically alternate (tension–compression) to maintain equilibrium perpendicular to the chords.

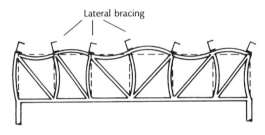

In-plane buckling of truss members

8.9.1.1 Depth/span ratio

The principle of dilution of material appears to suggest that the larger the structural depth, the higher the structural efficiency. It has been shown in the case of beams that, beyond a certain optimal value, increase in structural depth increases weight (6.3.2.3). The same principle applies to trusses. Although forces in the chords decrease with increasing depth, forces in the webs are practically unchanged, and increasing depth increases the lengths of these members. Approximately half the web members are in compression and increasing their lengths reduces their efficiency due to the increased susceptibility to buckling.

An optimal depth/span ratio for a planar truss is approximately $\frac{1}{10}$.

8.9.2 Vierendeel

Another way of discretising the beam is into non triangular cells, e.g. rectangular. This configuration is known as a **Vierendeel** beam or frame (after the Belgian engineer who first introduced it in 1896). The members of this structure, which is highly statically indeterminate, are subject to both direct action (axial forces) and flexure. This is a typical example of a mixed action structure (7.6.2).

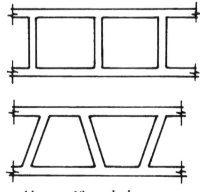

Dilution of beam – Vierendeel

8.9.2.1 The nature and magnitude of axial forces can easily be computed (for example the chord forces are equal to the simply supported beam moment divided by the structural depth – the distance between the chords).

The moment distribution is more complex as the structure is highly redundant statically. A qualitative appreciation of the bending action can be derived by reference to the deformed shape.

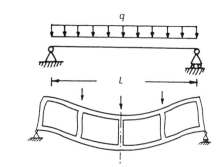

Deflected shape

8.9.2.2 The Vierendeel beam can be further 'diluted' into a truss or into a secondary Vierendeel. In the first case, the whole structure is subject to a direct action mode, with individual members subjected only to axial forces. In the second case (secondary Vierendeel) a secondary flexural action still exists.

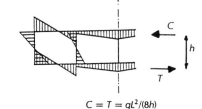

$$C = T = qL^2/(8h)$$

Moment diagram

8.9.2.3 It is difficult to postulate a 'rule of thumb' for the span/depth ratio of a Vierendeel frame. This structural system is applicable in either steel or concrete. The stiffness depends not just on the structural depth but also on the stiffness of the individual members. Span/depth ratios in the range of $\frac{1}{8}-\frac{1}{10}$ are typical.

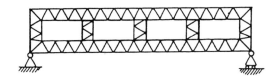

Vierendeel truss

8.10 Planar frames

A *Planar frame* or *Plane frame* is a planar structure consisting of rigidly jointed members acting primarily in flexure. The continuous beam and the Vierendeel beam are examples of planar frames. Planar frames are, with rare exceptions, statically indeterminate.

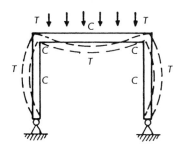

Bent

8.10.1 Simple, single cell frames

One of the simplest forms of frame is a single cell consisting of two columns and a rigidly connected beam. This configuration is sometimes referred to as a **Bent** (since it can be formed by 'bending' a single bar).

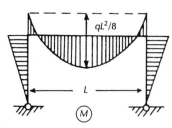

Moment diagram

Some variations in which the 'beam' is constructed as two members forming a peaked roof configuration are sometimes referred to as *Portal frames* or *Gable frames*.

8.10.1.1 The main action of such a frame is as a spanning structure similar to a single span beam. The structural depth is the depth of the beam. However, the rigid joints at the columns are subject to rotation and this rotation transmits bending into the columns. Bending moments can be appreciated by reference to the deflected shape.

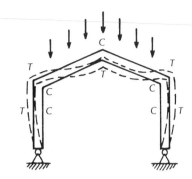

Gable (portal) frame

8.10.1.2 Frames are often subject to *Sway* or 'side sway' as it is sometimes referred to, particularly under the action of horizontal loads such as result from wind and earthquake. In this regard the frame acts essentially as a cantilever from the ground.

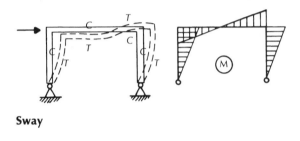

Sway

8.10.2 Multi-cell frames

The concept of the single cell frame can be extended horizontally to form a *Multi-bay frame*, analogous to the continuous beam, and/or vertically to form a *Multi-storey frame*. As the height of the frame relative to its width increases, the major action mode changes from spanning to cantilever. In high-rise multi-storey buildings, the main framing design problem is resistance to horizontal rather than gravity loads.

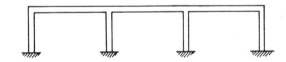

Multi-bay frame

8.10.2.1 Span/depth ratio
The equivalent span of the beam of a planar frame (for estimating its depth) varies, depending on the relative stiffness of the columns and beam. For relatively long, narrow columns, the situation approaches the simply supported case. At the other extreme – short, thick columns – the fixed-ended beam case applies. In intermediate cases an intelligent estimate is normally sufficient as a first guess. Values of 0.7–0.8 of the spans are suitable for most cases.

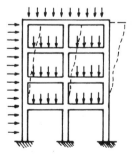

Multi-storey frame

8.11 Planar light-weight roof systems

Light-weight roofs are normally constructed of
steel. They contain several components. Starting
with the top layer the main components are:

❑ *Roof sheeting*, usually made of galvanised steel
  with some profilation to give it flexural stiffness
  (structural depth).
❑ The sheeting is supported on *Purlins*, which are
  light-weight beams, often made of *Cold-formed
  sections* – shapes bent from sheet steel (6.2.1).

The depth of cold-formed roof purlins is usually of
the order of 1/30 of the equivalent span, but
strength considerations mostly govern and these
depend on loads (snow and wind), which vary with
geographic location.

❑ The purlins are supported on the main load
  bearing component which may be a truss, a
  beam or a frame.
❑ *Wind bracing*. The elements listed above are
  designed primarily for gravity loads. In order
  to stabilise the structure to horizontal forces,
  particularly wind, bracing members are added
  which turn all the roof and wall surfaces into
  geometrically rigid *diaphragms* (see Chapter 9).
  The bracing system in fact turns the structure
  into a spatial structure for the purpose of
  stability analysis.
      Wind bracing also serves, in conjunction with
  the purlins, to provide lateral bracing for the
  chord or flange of the main bearing element –
  truss, beam etc.

It should also be noted that wind loads on light-
weight roofs often cause *Uplift*, the upward load
on the roof caused by wind suction (2.1.4), which
exceeds the dead load, so that the net load is
upwards. This load reversal has to be allowed for
in the design. Members in tension under gravity
load may act in compression under wind load and
are then subject to buckling.

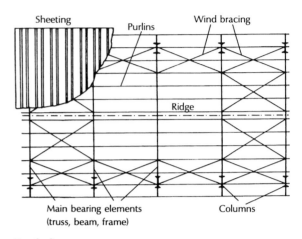

Roof plan

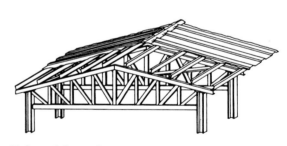

Light-weight roof

Geometry	Action mode	
	Direct	**Flexure**
Discrete		
Continuous	\n\n**Column**	

9 Cables and Arches

This chapter deals with a special type of spanning planar structure, consisting of a single member in direct action (tension or compression). It introduces the concept of *funicular shape* and the principles governing it. It is a fundamental principle in structural engineering as it involves the natural flow of forces in the form of tension or compression – the fundamental forces.

9.1 Funicular shape

The **Funicular shape** of a load over a span is the shape a member with no flexural stiffness (such as a rope or a chain) would take under the given load if it was suspended over the span with its ends fixed (*funiculus* is rope in Latin).

Note: **The funicular shape is a function of the load alone.**

9.1.1 Cable

It is intuitively apparent that the rope or chain mentioned above is in **pure tension** (the rope can take neither bending nor compression). A structure in pure tension having the funicular shape of its load is termed a **Cable** (see also 8.2 for a definition relating to the composition of a cable).

9.1.1.1 Since a cable has no flexural stiffness it automatically adjusts itself to the applied load as the load changes, and always assumes the funicular shape.

> This is the reason it is used in the indirect but intuitive definition above. A more rigorous definition is: a funicular shape is the shape of a member bridging over the span subject to the given load and acting in pure tension or in pure compression. Yet another definition, involving the concept of moment diagram, is given further down.

Funicular shapes

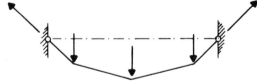

Cable equilibrium

9.1.1.2 A cable is an **unstable** structure. If the load changes drastically, for example reverses direction, deflections can be unacceptably large. However, if the possible range of load variation is small, the structure may be stable within this range (see 7.2 for a definition of stability), and then it is deformable (7.3). *Suspension bridges* are an example of such structures. The weight of the bridge by far exceeds any variable load and the structure is generally stable.

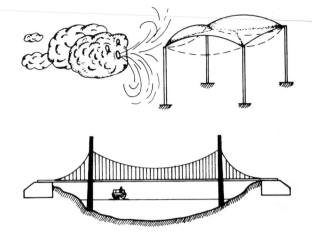

A well known exception was the Tacoma Narrows suspension bridge, in Washington State in the USA. The bridge collapsed and fell into the Puget Sound on 7 November 1940, when it entered resonant oscillations under a 67 km/h wind. Since then, aerodynamic considerations play a central role in suspension bridge design.

Suspension bridge

9.1.2 Arch

Let us now 'invert' the shape of a cable under a given load, that is the *sag* at any point is turned into a *rise*. The point is now above the chord joining the end points, by the same amount it was previously below it.

A structure built according to the new shape is now in **pure compression**. A structure built according to the funicular shape in compression is termed an *Arch*.

9.1.2.1 Since an arch acts in compression, it **must possess flexural stiffness**, in order to resist buckling. This flexural stiffness turns it into a rigid structure (as opposed to the deformable cable), so that its **shape is fixed** and cannot adapt itself to a changing load. Consequently **the arch acts in pure compression only under the load for which it is the funicular shape**. Under any other load the action is a combination of axial compression and flexure.

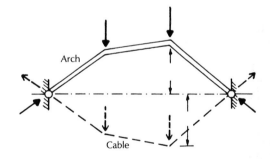

Note that the definition of an arch is a **structural** one, not geometrical. Here again the relation structure–shape comes into play. **Not every structure that looks like an arch is one**. For a structure to be an arch certain conditions have to be satisfied which link the geometry with the flow of internal forces. **False arches abound** in our built environment. The topic is pursued further in the following sections.

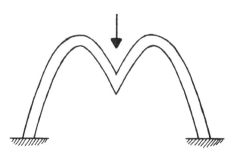

This is not an arch!

9.2 Forces in cables and arches

A structure which bridges over a span and has the funicular shape of the given load can be an arch or a cable (depending on whether the shape is the compressive or the tensile shape), or it can be a beam. What makes a funicular structure capable of bridging a span in tension or in compression, as opposed to a beam having the same shape, is the capability of both supports to sustain horizontal reaction components, as demonstrated in the following examples.

9.2.1 Example – cable

Consider a cable loaded by a concentrated load at its centre. Looking at a free-body diagram of half the cable (excluding the load), the overturning moment is produced by the vertical components of the reaction and the cable tension, which form a couple of forces $P/2$ with lever arm $L/2$. The stabilising moment is produced by the horizontal components of the reaction and the cable force, forming a couple of forces H with the lever arm h – the **Sag**. The sag of the cable at a point is the vertical distance of that point from the chord connecting the supports.

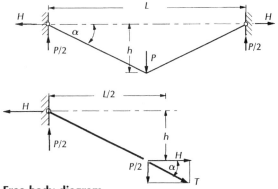

Free-body diagram

9.2.1.1 Calculation of the horizontal component H and of the cable tension T is straightforward. From moment equilibrium:

$$\sum M = 0 \Rightarrow H \times h - (P/2) \times (L/2) = 0$$

$$\Rightarrow H = \frac{PL}{4h}$$

$$T = (P/2)/\sin \alpha = \sqrt{(P/2)^2 + H^2}$$

$$= \sqrt{(P/2)^2 + (PL/4h)^2} = (P/2)\sqrt{1 + (L/2h)^2}$$

9.2.1.2 The two important conclusions from the analysis are:

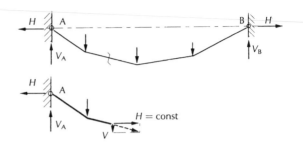

- ❑ **The structural depth of a cable (or arch) is its sag (rise).** The sag of a cable is the maximum sag (see below for rise of an arch). Compare this result to a beam whose structural depth is the depth of the member.
- ❑ **The horizontal component of the internal force is constant along the cable (arch)**, provided that the applied loads are vertical. This is a simple result of horizontal force equilibrium: $\sum H = 0$, since the couple forming forces H constitutes the only horizontal components in any free-body diagram.

Free-body diagram

9.2.2 Example – arch

Consider an arch loaded with a uniformly distributed load. **Note**: The load is uniformly distributed over the horizontal projection, for example a snow load, see 2.1.4.1. The analysis is similar to the cable example. The horizontal couple H with lever arm h, the **Rise** of the free-body diagram, balances the overturning couple $qL/2$ with lever arm $L/4$. The rise is the vertical distance of a point on the arch from the chord connecting its supports. The rise of the arch is the maximum rise.

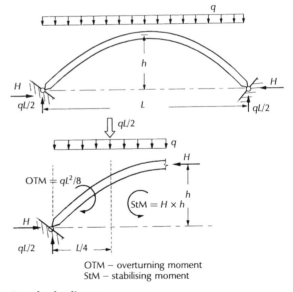

OTM – overturning moment
StM – stabilising moment

Free-body diagram

9.2.2.1 Force analysis is very similar to that of the simply supported beam of section 4.2. The shear force at mid span vanishes, the reaction is equal to the load resultant – $qL/2$. Moment equilibrium yields the value of the horizontal force H:

$$\sum M = 0 \Rightarrow H \times h - (qL/2) \times (L/4) = 0$$

$$\Rightarrow H = \frac{qL^2}{8h}$$

The difference between an arch and a curved structure which is **not an arch** can now be clearly understood. The difference between an arch and a beam, curved to the same shape, is that the beam has a roller at one end and therefore cannot develop horizontal reactions.

The implication of this 'little difference' is tremendous. The arch, acting in direct action, has its full rise as its structural depth, whereas the beam has just its own depth and would therefore result in a much heavier design.

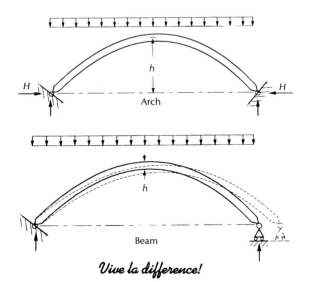

9.3 Funicular shape and moment diagram

We have seen that both the funicular shape and the shape of the moment diagram are functions of the load. Furthermore, if we look at the expressions for the moment at mid span of a simply supported beam and for the horizontal force of a cable or arch of the same span we observe a close similarity:

Uniformly	beam:	$M = qL^2/8$
distributed load:	funicular:	$H = qL^2/8h$
Point load:	beam:	$M = PL/4$
	funicular:	$H = PL/4h$

The similarity is not coincidental. The overturning moment is the same in both cases. The stabilising moment is provided by the bending moment M in the case of the beam (4.2.2.6), and by the couple $H \times h$ in the case of the funicular shape.

The same is true if we consider any cross-section along the beam, and along the funicular shape, if we replace h by the ordinate y of the funicular shape relative to the chord. We can express y in terms of the moment (which varies with the location, x) and the horizontal force H which is constant along the arch:

$$y(x) = \frac{M(x)}{H}$$

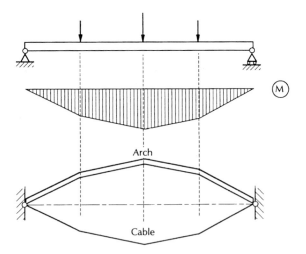

This result can form a basis for an alternative definition of funicular shape: funicular shape of a given load over a given span is the shape of the moment diagram of a simply supported beam of the same span loaded by the same load.

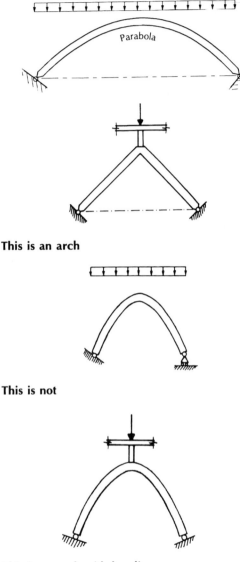

9.3.1 Some results

☐ If the moment diagram is drawn on the **tension** side of the beam it has the shape of the corresponding **cable**, and vice versa, if the moment diagram is drawn on the **compression** side of the beam, it has the shape of the corresponding **arch**.

☐ The funicular shape of a load uniformly distributed over a horizontal projection is a **parabola**.

☐ The moment diagram of a simply supported beam under a given load, when drawn on the tension side, has the shape of a cable of the same span loaded by the same load. This result can help in drawing moment diagrams. See, for instance the continuous beam in 8.5.

9.3.1.1 The difference between a 'true arch' and a 'false arch' (or rather a non arch) is now relatively easy to see. **What makes an arch an arch is: (1) support conditions enabling horizontal reaction; (2) correspondence of the shape with the load.**

Here the **structure–shape** or **force–form** relation finds its utmost expression. Keeping 'true to form' will avoid the **arch–arc** confusion, at least on the semantic/syntactic level. (Not every arc is an arch, and vice versa.)

9.3.2 Principal stress

9.3.2.1 Funicular structures can be considered 'pure structures', in the sense that the internal forces in the member are purely one of the fundamental direct actions – tension or compression.

It was mentioned in Chapter 3 (3.7.1) that force analysis can be performed in terms of tension and compression without recourse to other types of forces, such as shear forces. The way this can be done for a beam is as follows.

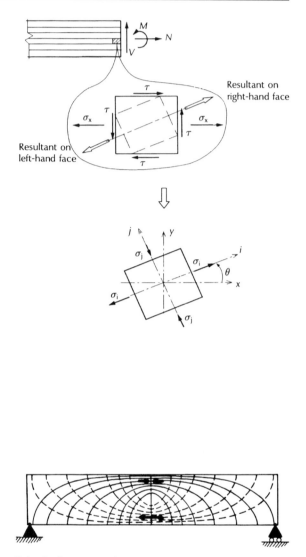

9.3.2.2 The description of internal forces in a beam as a combination of axial forces, shear forces and bending moment, or, in terms of stress, as a combination of normal and shear stresses, is simply a matter of convenience. It results from the orientation of the cross-section – perpendicular to the axis of the member and of the 'fibres'.

If we take a small fibre particle with its normal and shear stress and start rotating it, we find that the magnitude of shear and normal stress changes, so as to maintain the resultant force on the rotated face unchanged.

Continuing this rotation we can reach an orientation in which the shear stress vanishes altogether, and the particle is subject to normal stresses only – tension and/or compression (note that if the shear vanishes on one face, it must vanish on all faces, to maintain equilibrium). Yet the particle is the same particle in the same beam subject to the same resultant forces. The two stress configurations – one with and one without shear stress – are, therefore, completely equivalent. The normal stresses which fully describe the state of stress at a point are termed *Principal stresses*, and the directions of these stresses are *Principal axes*.

Principal stress trajectories in a simply supported beam

9.3.2.3 If the principal stresses and axes are plotted for points at close intervals over the beam we obtain principal *Stress trajectories*. The principal stress trajectories of a beam form two families of mutually perpendicular curves. The curves representing the tensile stress resemble cables, while those representing compression resemble arches.

9.3.2.4 Although it is always possible to express the state of stress in terms of principal stresses, it is not always convenient, or useful, for design purposes. Sometimes specific orientations are dictated by the physical configuration of the structure, particularly at connections or at contact surfaces between elements or material. Such contact surfaces are often subject to shear forces and have to be designed for this action – see, for example, composite slab systems (8.8.1).

9.4 Supports of arches and cables

The supports of arches and cables must resist the horizontal forces relayed to them by the structure. This can be a major problem when the supports are above ground level. Indeed, this was the major problem in historical arch construction when construction materials (stone) could not support significant bending or tension.

9.4.1 Arch support

One way of solving the problem of supporting an elevated arch is through a tension rod connecting the two supports. Often this is not a desirable solution and other solutions have been adopted throughout history, such as heavy abutments, flying buttresses, sloping columns, cascading arches and the like.

9.4.1.1 Note that, since the horizontal force in an arch is constant, and any segment of the arch is in equilibrium under the applied load, it follows that any segment 'cut' from a given arch and translated to a different location will have the same horizontal force components, under the same load. This enables a complex arrangement of arches such that horizontal force components of joining segments 'cancel out', allowing the vertical resultant to be taken by a simple column.

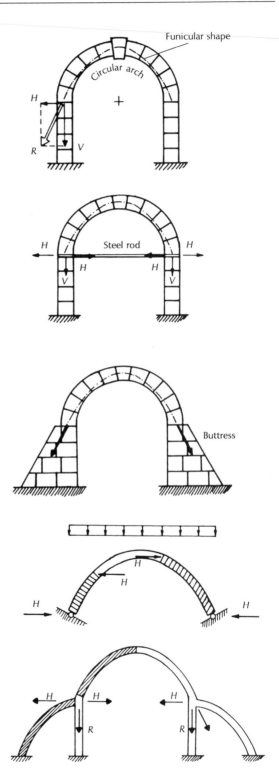

9.4.2 *Cable support*

In the case of cables, the horizontal forces at the support are often balanced by adjoining anchorage cables, while the vertical resultant of the two cables is taken by a *Post*. The main problem is the anchorage in the ground where there is a considerable vertical component pulling up. The massive *Anchor blocks* of suspension bridges are a typical example.

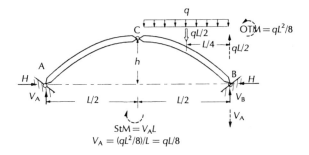

Anchor block

9.5 Arch analysis – bending moments

As mentioned above, when the load on the arch does not correspond to the funicular shape of the arch, the arch is subject to bending moments.

The *Two-pinned arch* analysed above is statically indeterminate and the bending moments cannot be analysed based on equilibrium alone. (In the analysis above we took advantage of the assumption of the vanishing of the bending moment and shear force.)

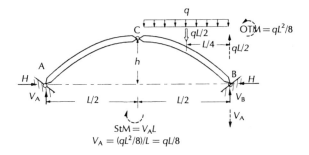

$$OTM = qL^2/8$$

$$StM = V_A L$$
$$V_A = (qL^2/8)/L = qL/8$$

9.5.1 *Three-pinned arch*

A *Three-pinned arch* is statically determinate. It can be analysed as follows.

9.5.1.1 Take a free-body diagram from a support to the interior hinge. The equilibrium of the free-body diagram together with the equilibrium of the arch as a whole (three equations each, six altogether) enables computation of the four reaction components and two internal hinge forces (there is no moment at the hinge).

Free-body diagrams from a support to any other cross-section then enable computation of the normal force, shear force and bending moment at the cross-section.

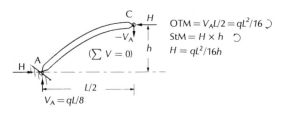

$$OTM = V_A L/2 = qL^2/16$$
$$StM = H \times h$$
$$H = qL^2/16h$$

$$(\sum V = 0)$$

$$V_A = qL/8$$

Free-body diagram

9.5.1.2 A more direct, graphic or semi-graphic method of obtaining the whole moment diagram is as follows:

❑ Plot the moment diagram of the simply supported beam of the same span as the arch. **Plot the diagram on the compression side** of the beam so that it looks like an arch.
❑ Superimpose on the moment diagram thus constructed a graph of the arch (say a parabola if it is a parabolic arch), scaled in such a way that the two diagrams intersect at the three hinges.
❑ The moment diagram of the arch, **plotted on the compression side** of the scaled line diagram of the arch, is the difference between the two curves. Note that moments are measured vertically between the two curves.

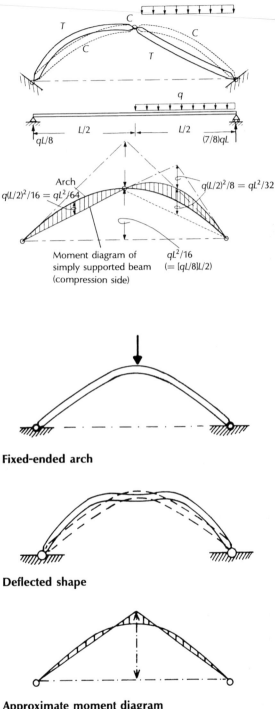

9.5.2 Approximate analysis

Approximate moment diagrams for a two-pinned arch and a **Fixed-ended arch** can be drawn in a similar way and with reference to the deflected shape:

❑ Draw the moment diagram of the load for the corresponding simply supported beam as above.
❑ Draw a scaled line diagram of the arch and 'play' with it, shifting it up and down as necessary and scaling it to an approximate scale, so that the bending moment alternates sides in a way corresponding to the intuitive deflected shape. The diagrams cross each other at points of inflexion, such that the simply supported beam moment diagram is always on the concave side of the arch line diagram. Ensure zero moments at hinges and non zero moments at fixed ends.

Fixed-ended arch

Deflected shape

Approximate moment diagram

❑ A qualitative moment diagram is the diagram
bounded by the two curves (drawn on the compression side of the arch).

9.6 Arch stability

An arch, as a compressed element, is subject to
buckling. The buckling can take place sideways,
perpendicular to the plane of the arch, or in the
plane of the arch, depending on the relative stiffness of the two directions.

    The lateral buckling (sideways) is generally
more critical since the buckling length for a two-
pinned arch is the full length of the arch (8.1.1.2).
The in-plane buckling length, on the other hand, is
approximately half the arch length (and similarly
for a three-pinned arch).

    Assuming lateral buckling is restrained, the
cross-section dimensions of an arch are governed
by in-plane buckling and by bending (when the
load does not correspond to the funicular shape).
The optimal rise-to-span ratio for an arch is in the
range $\frac{1}{6}$–$\frac{1}{4}$. The depth-to-span ratio of the arch is
usually in the range $\frac{1}{40}$–$\frac{1}{70}$.

9.6.1 Arch buckling modes

There are two in-plane overall buckling modes
for arches. The most common mode for 'deep
arches' (rise-to-span ratio greater than approximately $\frac{1}{6}$) is buckling inward at one side and
outward at the other.

9.6.1.1 For shallow arches (rise to depth smaller
than approximately $\frac{1}{8}$) there is a buckling mode
termed **Snap-through buckling**, which is due to the
elastic shortening of the arch.

    In shallow arches a relatively small axial short-
ening can cause significant vertical deflection which
reduces the arch's rise, increasing the compressive force and thus increasing axial shortening.

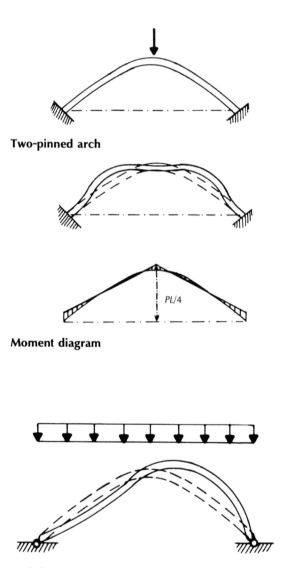

Two-pinned arch

Moment diagram

$PL/4$

Arch buckling (in plane)

The result is a progressive flattening of the arch until it 'snaps through' turning, in effect into a cable, with a sag similar to the original rise.

In deep arches these effects are considered secondary, but in shallow arches they may govern the behaviour. A non linear (computer) analysis is required to compute the buckling load in this mode.

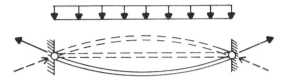

Snap-through buckling

9.6.1.2 When an arch is loaded by a concentrated load, particularly if it has a small thickness, a local buckling can occur in the shape of a dimple (local snap through). Such local buckling may lead to general buckling through a process of *progressive collapse*.

9.7 Barrel vault

A *Barrel vault* is an arch with a large width (perpendicular to the arch's plane). The relation of a barrel vault to an arch is similar to the relation of a one-way slab to a beam (8.7). If we cut a narrow strip from the vault across the span we obtain an arch, and since this strip is representative of all such strips the vault is in fact a planar structure, analysed as an arch.

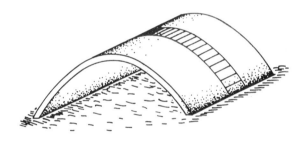

Barrel vault

The supports of a barrel vault are continuous along the width or at close intervals so there is no significant spanning in the direction perpendicular to the span of the arch.

A barrel vault can buckle only in its plane due to its large lateral stiffness. Local buckling is possible in thin-skinned vaults.

9.8 Braced arch

In the same way that a beam is discretised into a truss, an arch can be discretised into a reticulated arch or *Braced arch*.

Such an arch is typical of many arch bridges, with the roadway either suspended from the arch

(for example Sydney Harbour bridge) or bearing over it (less common for steel arches). The roadway can also be partly suspended from, and partly supported on, the arch. Barrel vaults can also be constructed as reticulated steel structures, in the form of a **Braced barrel vault** (see also braced shell, Chapter 11).

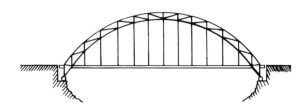

Braced arch

Discretisation of the arch into a Vierendeel arch is possible but not common.

In addition to overall buckling of the arch, buckling of individual members (between joints), both laterally and in-plane, needs to be considered in the design of braced arches and barrel vaults.

Geometry	Action mode	
	Direct	**Flexure**
Discrete		
Continuous		

10 Introduction to Spatial Structures

From the geometrical point of view, it is possible to extend planar structure configurations to spatial structures, simply by adding a dimension. The extension can often be done in several ways, so the range of spatial structures is much larger than that of planar structures.

From the structural point of view, however, the extension often involves, not merely the addition of a third dimension, but a conceptual change in the way the structures act, so that while the shape of a spatial structure can be similar to that of a planar structure (e.g. a cylindrical shell and a barrel vault), their mode of action may be radically different.

10.1 Action in spatial structures

We have defined two major modes of action for planar bar structures – direct action and flexure. In order to extend these concepts to spatial structures of continuous geometry, we need to consider a typical 'element' of such structures. Reticulated spatial structures consist of bars, so that the concepts relating to bars of planar structures are also applicable to spatial bar structures, with the addition of *torsion* (see 10.1.2 below).

If a planar structure is represented by linear elements, a continuous spatial structure is essentially a **surface**, consisting of 'surface elements'. However while bars are actual physical elements, surface elements are fictitious; they are, in fact, three-dimensional free-body diagrams 'cut' (figuratively) from the surface. Usually (but not essentially) the cuts would be quadrilateral to show internal forces in two orthogonal directions.

10.1.1 Direct action

In planar structures, direct action involves axial forces stretching or compressing the member

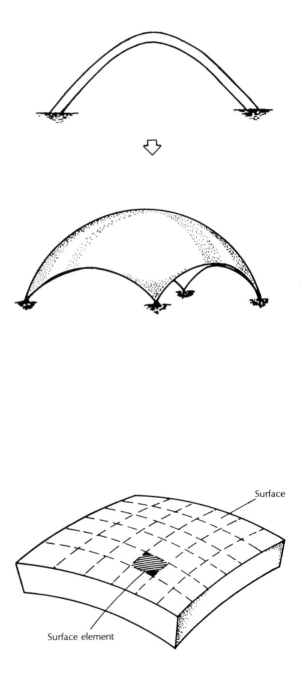

Surface

Surface element

along its length. By analogy direct action in spatial structures involves *Normal forces*, which are internal forces perpendicular to the 'cut' face, tending to stretch or compress the element within the surface, or to stretch the element in one direction and compress it in the other.

In addition, direct action also includes **shear forces** which distort the shape of the element (turning the rectangle into a parallelogram). In other words, direct action involves any forces which affect motion **within the surface**, but not laterally to it.

Note the orientation of shear forces: forces on parallel cross-sections form a couple. The orientation of the two couples must be so that they are in equilibrium – the net moment vanishes, consequently the forces at each corner are directed either towards the corner or away from it. This is similar to shear stresses (and forces) in bar structures (5.7.1.2).

This direct mode of action is termed *Membrane action*, and the internal forces complying with it are *Membrane forces*.

It has been mentioned (9.3.2) that shear stresses in flexure can be disposed of by rotating the element to its **principal axes** orientation. The same is true for the shear forces in membrane action: the element can be rotated to its principal axes at which only normal forces act.

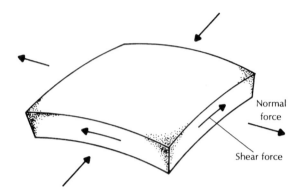

Membrane forces

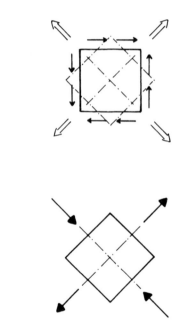

Principal axes

10.1.2 Flexure

Flexure involves forces which cause lateral deformation of the surface, namely, deflections from the original unstressed surface, normal to it. These forces, as in planar structures involve bending normal to the boundary faces of the element, and lateral shear forces.

10.1.2.1 In addition to the couples normal to the cut planes, which cause bending, flexure in spatial structures (including bar structures) may involve couples **within** the cut plane, which cause *Torsion* – an action which distorts the cut surface from a rectangle (roughly) into a parallelogram (roughly). It also rotates two parallel sections relative to each other, twisting the surface. The moment causing torsion is called *Torque*.

Torsion involves shear stresses distributed in a similar way to the normal stresses caused by bending (5.7.1.2). Torsion applies also to members of reticulated spatial structure acting in flexure (e.g. beam grid).

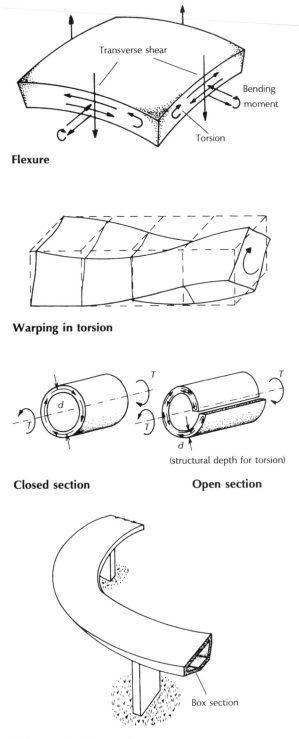

Flexure

Warping in torsion

Closed section   (structural depth for torsion)

Open section

The phenomenon of torsion is considerably more complex than bending, as the deformations involved include *Warping* – distortion of the cross-section out of plane, so that planar sections no longer remain planar, as in bending. This can be demonstrated by inscribing a straight line on a common eraser and then twisting the eraser. The line twists out of straightness.

Torsion is often combined with bending as an action mode. Torsion, as a principal action mode, is generally undesirable. Efficient design for torsion often conflicts with efficient design for bending. While bending requires spreading material away from the neutral axis, in the bending plane, torsion requires as nearly circular sections as practical, namely spreading of material away from the centroid equally in all directions. Thin-walled open sections such as I or cold-formed sections, which are very efficient in bending, are extremely inefficient in torsion. The structural depth for torsion in these sections is limited within the thickness of the material. Concrete is particularly sensitive to torsion, which is associated with brittle failure mode in this material.

In cases where significant torsion is unavoidable, closed 'box' sections are often employed. Such sections offer an optimal combination of torsional and bending stiffness. Bridges and elevated roadways, which curve in a horizontal projection, are a typical example of such structures.

Bridge with horizontal curve

10.2 Spatial geometries

As mentioned, it is possible to extend planar geo-metries by adding a dimension in different ways, and it is always possible to 'dilute' (or discretise) a continuous structure into a reticulated structure.

The following table provides a 'bird's eye view' of some structural systems thus obtained. Definitions and more detailed descriptions are given in the remainder of this chapter, for structures of planar surfaces, and in following chapters for structures of curved surfaces.

Planar structure	Spatial structure (continuous)	Spatial structure (reticulated)
Bar in axial action	Plate (diaphragm)	Diaphragm truss
Beam, frame, truss	Two-way slab, folded plate	Grid, space truss, space frame
Pin-jointed network	Hinged-plate network, sponge lattice	Spatial pin-jointed network, braced polyhedral lattice
Arch	Dome, shell, plate dome, plate shell	Braced dome, braced shell
Cable	Fabric structure	Cable net

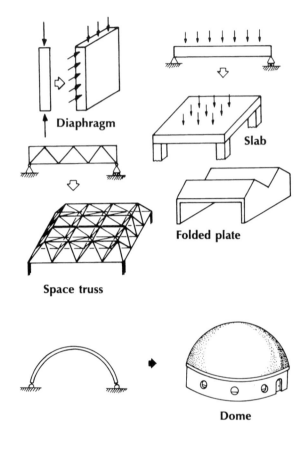

Diaphragm

Slab

Folded plate

Space truss

Dome

10.3 Plates

Plate
A **planar** surface in membrane action. For a planar surface to be in membrane action, it cannot be loaded perpendicular to its surface (this is not the case for curved surfaces).

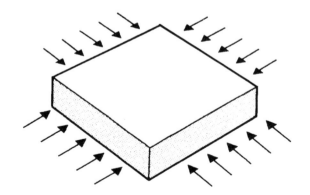

Plate

Diaphragm

A plate employed primarily in buildings for stiffening purposes.

The term 'plate' refers to a primary structural element, similar to the term 'bar'. Plate elements are often used in multi-element networks, consisting of many plates, or plates in combination with other elements, such as bars.

The term 'diaphragm' refers to a specific application of a plate as a single element, similar to a column in planar action. Although the diaphragm itself is, in fact, a planar structure, diaphragms are typically used as stiffening elements, enabling structures which act as planar structures under gravity loads to resist horizontal loads, in a spatial network.

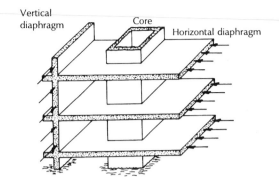

Concrete framed building

10.3.1 Diaphragms as stiffening elements

The skeleton of a building is often designed to support primarily the vertical gravity loads. Horizontal loads are often resisted by a system of horizontal and vertical diaphragms.

The horizontal diaphragms are normally provided by slabs, or roof surfaces, whose primary action under gravity loads is in bending (8.8, 8.11). Vertical diaphragms are provided by service cores or by stiffened walls. In concrete structures these are reinforced concrete walls (which may have openings). In steel framed structures wall stiffening is often achieved by **Cross bracing** between columns and beams, creating a vertical truss.

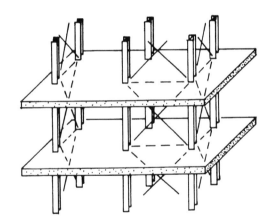

Cross bracing in steel framed building

10.3.2 Deep beam

When the ratio of the depth of a beam to its span is larger than about $\frac{1}{3}$, the simple beam model, presented in Chapter 4, is no longer valid. The **Deep beam** acts as a plate with a complex stress distribution. Local buckling may need to be considered in cases where the thickness of the plate is small relative to the depth.

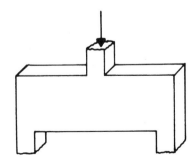

Deep beam

10.4 Folded plate

Folded plate

A folded plate is a spanning, area covering structure (usually a roof) consisting of a number of elongated plates, joined together along the long edges, across the span. This is an example of plate structure, in the same way that a truss is an example of bar structure.

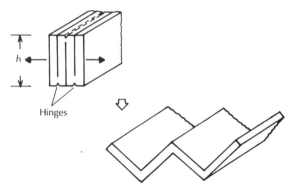

10.4.1 Geometric description

A folded plate is an example of **dilution of a beam** into a spatial structure with high structural depth but small thickness. It can be conceived as follows.

Start with a beam of the required structural depth (say $\frac{1}{10}$ of the span) and slice it into thin layers alternately from top and bottom, but not quite through – leaving thin unsliced portions at top and bottom.

Now grab two opposing edges of the beam across its width and spread them apart in a direction perpendicular to the span, with the narrow layers at the top and bottom serving as 'hinges'. The result is a 'fan fold' surface covering the whole width of the structure, without adding any material to the original beam.

Dilution of beam into folded plate

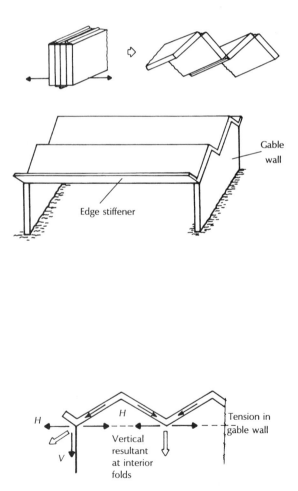

10.4.1.1 The structure can be made with actual hinges along the folds, so as to be a **foldable** as well as folded plate. This demonstrates the fact that the folded plate on its own is **unstable** (it can fold and unfold). In order to be stabilised, it needs to be **fixed** in its final shape along the opposing walls forming the supports – the *Gable walls* or *Gables*. The gable wall itself is a diaphragm wall.

The hinged connections between the plates are analogous to the pin joints of pin-jointed bar structures. Thus, plate structures can be constructed and analysed as hinge jointed or as rigid jointed, with similar idealisation assumptions as in the case of trusses (4.8.1, see also mode of action below).

10.4.1.2 The first and last plates of the folded plate structure possess long unsupported edges. Due to the small thickness of the plates the lateral stiffness of these edges is very low and they require *Edge stiffeners*. The edge stiffener usually takes the form of a narrow strip which generates an additional fold at the ends of the exterior plates. Such edge stiffeners are required along free edges of all thin walled structural elements (see *shells* in the next chapter).

10.4.2 Mode of action

On a large scale, the folded plate can be considered simply as a one-way slab or beam, having a folded cross-section, with compression at the top folds and tension at the bottom folds.

10.4.2.1 Looking more closely, however, it can be seen that the action is more complex, since the individual plates act, under applied distributed load, in bending (as one-way slabs) across their width, between folds. The folds serve as supports for this action. This action is similar to a truss, in which loads are applied along members and not just at nodes. As a result, the members – the plates in this case – act in flexure as a secondary mode of action, in addition to the primary, direct action – membrane action in this case.

Considering the primary action, the load can be regarded as a *Knife-edge load* – a uniformly distributed load along the fold lines. This load is resisted by internal forces within the plates in membrane action.

10.4.2.2 Folded plates are usually constructed in reinforced concrete. Prefabricated, precast and often prestressed folded plate segments are also available. The typical depth/span ratio ranges from $\frac{1}{15}$ to $\frac{1}{10}$.

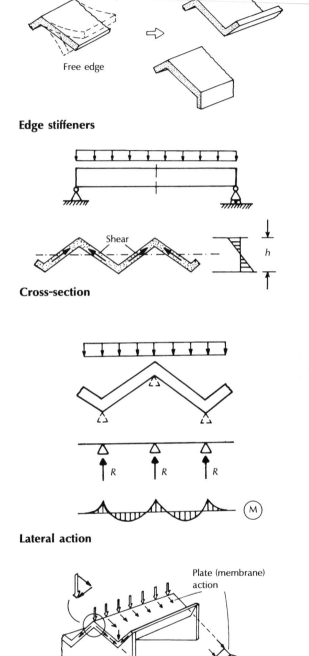

Free edge

Edge stiffeners

Cross-section

Lateral action

Plate (membrane) action

Gable wall

Longitudinal action

10.4.2.3 Folded plates can be discretised and constructed in steel as bar structures, where each plate is constructed as a truss. The membrane forces are then resolved into axial compression and tension forces in the bars. Each plate is analysed for the primary action as a planar truss, loaded with the components of the knife-edge load lying in its plane. The lateral bending (due to the lateral distributed load) needs also to be taken into account, in both chord and web members. Span/depth ratios for reticulated folded plates are similar to solid configurations.

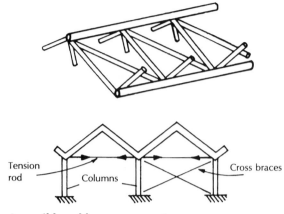

A possible gable arrangement

If the folds are actually hinged, the maximum lateral bending moment in the plates is $ql^2/8$, where l is the horizontal projection of the plate width. If, as is more often the case in concrete structures, the folds are actually rigid jointed, the lateral bending action is like a continuous beam (8.5), with the folds forming the supports. However, the folds are, in fact, elastic supports, particularly near mid span, allowing some spread-out of the plates. This causes the bending moments across the plates to alter, an effect which needs to be taken into account, particularly in relatively shallow structures.

10.4.3 Folded plate structures

Any spanning structure can be executed as a folded plate, for instance frames and arches (barrel vaults). In the latter case, the curve of the arch is replaced with straight segments. A large variety of geometries exists in the literature.

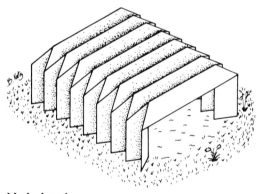

Folded plate frame

10.5 Two-way slabs

A *Two-way slab* is a planar surface spanning in two directions and acting in flexure. The slab is supported along the whole or part of the perimeter of the spanned area. There may be more than one span in any direction, in which case the slab is **continuous** over several spans.

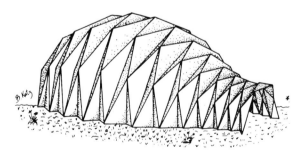

Folded shell (after O.L. Tonon[1])

10.5.1 Mode of action

A two-way slab action is produced if the shape of the spanned area is roughly regular (e.g. square, equilateral triangle or other polygon). The load on the slab 'splits' more or less equally between two orthogonal directions and therefore the two-way slab is more efficient than a one-way slab of similar span.

The deflected shape of a two-way slab is a doubly curved surface – there is curvature in both directions. As a result, the corners tend to 'lift off' the supports. If the corners are held down and prevented from lifting, torsion couples are produced in the corner regions, which stiffen the slab as a whole and reduce the deflection in the middle of the span. Looking along diagonal sections from the corners the deflected shape is that of a fixed-ended beam – the corners are effectively fixed, hence the increased stiffness.

The depth of a solid two-way slab is in the range $\frac{1}{30}-\frac{1}{35}$ of the effective span. The lesser of the two effective spans may be used. Slabs with triangular plans are particularly stiff. The effective span of a triangular slab may be assumed as the diameter of the inscribed circle.

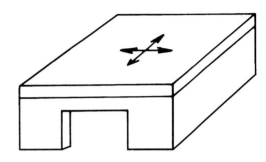

Two-way slab

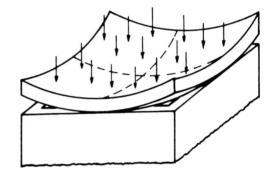

10.5.2 Flat plate

A two-way slab which is continuous over several spans can be supported directly on columns, rather than on continuous stiff supporting elements, such as walls or beams.

A slab supported directly on columns is termed a *Flat plate*. It acts somewhat differently to a slab on continuous supports.

10.5.2.1 The stiffness of a flat plate is lower and the deflections larger than in a continuously supported slab of the same thickness, due to the absence of stiff elements between the columns.

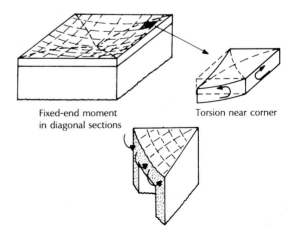

Fixed-end moment
in diagonal sections

Torsion near corner

Strips along column lines – *Column strips* – are more highly stressed than strips near mid spans –*Middle strips* – because the column strips serve as 'hidden', elastic supports for the middle strips.

A typical depth of a solid flat plate is $\frac{1}{22}-\frac{1}{18}$ of the effective span.

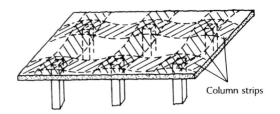

Flat plate

10.5.2.2 One of the main problems associated with flat plates is the problem of *Penetration* of columns through the plate, due to the high concentrated reaction force (there have been several cases of failure). To mitigate this problem without adding to the thickness of the slab, *Column capitals* are sometimes employed – thickening of the slab around the columns. The capitals are sometimes styled and left exposed for architectural effect. Such slabs are sometimes called *Mushroom slabs*.

Column penetration

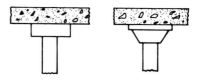

Column capitals

10.6 Dilution of the two-way slab

10.6.1 Two-way ribbed slab

A two-way ribbed slab can be formed by generating ribs in two directions, in the same way that a one-way ribbed slab is generated from its solid counterpart by concentrating material in closely spaced ribs (8.7.1).

A two-way ribbed slab is less rigid than a solid slab, because the torsional stiffness of the ribs is small so that little restraint is generated at the corners. The situation is different if ribs are inclined 45° to the boundaries, an arrangement which increases the stiffness. The restraint is then obtained in bending rather than torsion.

A three-way ribbed slab can be formed for triangular or hexagonal layouts in a similar way. Such a slab is extremely stiff and efficient, but difficult to execute.

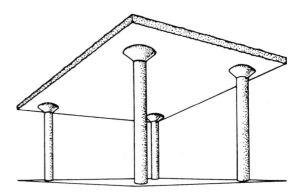

Mushroom slab

The spaces between ribs in two-way ribbed slabs are often left empty, without infill bodies and with the ribs exposed. Such slabs are termed *Hollow slabs* (UK) or *Waffle slabs* (US). The ribs and hollows are often formed by prefabricated units of varying materials and finishes.

Typical depths of two-way ribbed slabs supported on continuous stiff supports are in the range of $\frac{1}{30}$–$\frac{1}{25}$ of the lesser effective span.

10.6.1.1 In flat plate ribbed or hollow slab construction, column capitals are often generated simply by filling in (with concrete) the spaces between ribs around the column. It is possible to fill in the whole of the column strips with concrete, thus considerably stiffening the slab, but in this case the slab is no longer considered a flat plate but a slab with *Flat beams*.

Typical depths of flat plate ribbed slabs are in the range of $\frac{1}{20}$–$\frac{1}{17}$ of the lesser effective span.

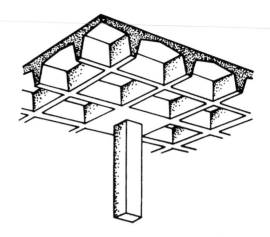

Hollow (waffle) slab

10.6.2 Beam grid

A *Beam grid*, or simply 'grid', is a discretisation of a two-way slab, obtained by concentrating material in beams running in two (or three) directions. The difference between a beam grid and a hollow slab is that the spacing of the beams is larger, and the space between the beam may be empty (without a slab) or covered with a (two-way) slab or with some light-weight structure (roof). The beams are subject to torsion as well as to bending.

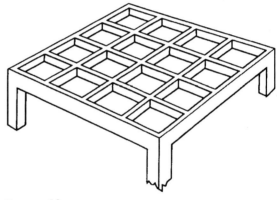

Beam grid

10.7 Slab discretisation – space trusses

Discretising a two- or three-way slab or beam grid into bar structures acting in direct (axial) action generates a *Space truss* or *Spatial truss*. The discretisation can be achieved in many ways. Details of some geometries and ways of implementation are discussed below.

The simplest form of space truss is a discretisation of the beams in a beam grid, or the ribs in a

Diagonal grid

ribbed slab, into a network of intersecting planar trusses. Such a grid of trusses is sometimes termed a *Lattice space truss*.

10.7.1 Double-layer grids

The two- or three-way slab can be discretised into spatial trusses in a large variety of geometries which are given the common term of *Double-layer grids*.

10.7.1.1 A double-layer grid consists of an upper and lower network of bars – the **chords**, interconnected by the **web** members. The two layers forming the chords can be any plane-filling pattern, and the patterns of the two layers need not be identical, though they need to be compatible.

If the two layers are identical, they are **offset** relative to each other. If they were not, a lattice truss would be generated instead of a double-layer grid.

The jargon used to identify double-layer grid configurations is as follows. The top layer geometry is named first followed by the word 'on' and the bottom layer geometry. If the two are identical the word 'offset' is sometimes added to emphasise it is a double-layer grid and not a lattice truss. For square chords, two orientations are distinguished – 'square' implies chord members are parallel with the boundary or column layout, 'diagonal' is used to indicate that chord members are inclined 45° to the boundary.

Examples: 'Square on square (offset)' – this is the most popular configuration in constructed structures to date; 'Square on diagonal', 'Diagonal on square'; 'Square on larger square'. The last three mentioned configurations are highly efficient, since they generate higher bar density for the compression, buckling prone chord (usually the top chord). There are some three-way grids. 'Triangle on triangle (offset)'; 'Triangle on hexagon'.

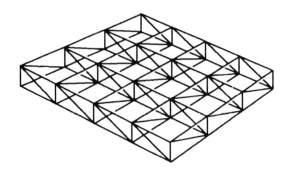

Lattice truss

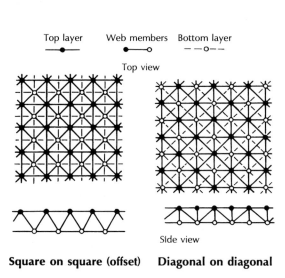

Square on square (offset)   **Diagonal on diagonal**

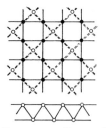 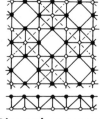

Square on diagonal   **Diagonal on square**

10.7.1.2 One of the features of double-layer grids is the regularity of their geometry. This feature makes them suitable for prefabrication. There exist today over a hundred firms specialising in the prefabrication of double-layer grid space truss systems worldwide.

A large variety of technical solutions exist for the main problem – the joining of a large number of members. The best known and probably most wide spread type of system is the 'ball joint' – tubular member, the best known of which is the 'Mero' system. Other systems aim at more economical assembly methods, sometimes at the expense of 'pleasing appearance'. Some systems are designed for the incorporation of specific roofing/surfacing products, such as glazing, with joint and member cross-section suitably configured.

10.7.1.3 From the structural behaviour point of view, the main problem in space truss design is buckling of compression members. The structure is statically indeterminate to a high degree and therefore susceptible to environmental effects (8.3.2). **Lack of fit** of members, in particular, causes **prestress** in the truss – forces present in members prior to loading. When members buckle in a brittle fashion (6.1.5, 8.1.1), the result is a susceptibility to *Progressive collapse* – the chain reaction of successive member buckling. At least one such spectacular failure has been reported (Hartford Coliseum, Hartford, Connecticut, 1978).

10.8 Space frames

It is possible to join together series of parallel planar frames in a three-dimensional network. The result is a space or spatial frame. In ordinary framed buildings there is no advantage in doing this, because the cooperation between frames in different planes is through torsion in the beams, an action for which most commonly used cross-sections are not efficient.

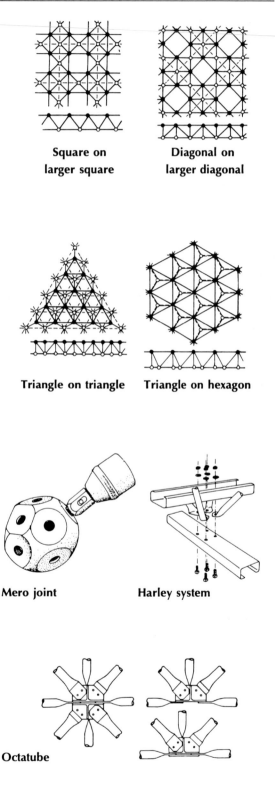

Square on larger square

Diagonal on larger diagonal

Triangle on triangle

Triangle on hexagon

Mero joint

Harley system

Octatube

There are, however, applications for which the use of a spatial frame is appropriate. One such application is in tall buildings where the spatial action of frames with closely spaced columns can be utilised.

10.8.1 Double-layer space frames

Another application of spatial frames is a **two-way Vierendeel** (or three-way). This structure is similar to a lattice space truss, or to a beam grid, but the web member layout is not diagonalised (does not form triangles), and therefore members are subject to bending and torsion, as well as to axial forces, similar to the planar counterpart.

The advantage of a space Vierendeel compared to a space truss is the lower density of bars and the simpler joints. There are prefabricated systems of two-way Vierendeel frames.

10.8.2 Polyhedral lattices

All spatial structures surveyed so far form surfaces, with structural depth confined in most cases within the thickness of the surface. The thickness itself does not serve a functional purpose (other than accommodating services etc.). It is possible to generate truly spatial, volume filling grids, the voids of which constitute the functional spaces, such as living spaces, halls etc. Such structures are extremely efficient, as they utilise the whole volume for structural depth, although members are often subject to flexure as well as axial action, when the network is not fully triangulated (see discussion in 11.6.2).

Other potential applications include mega-structures – structures covering very large spans (a small town or a city block, for example) or rising to very high levels (1 km or more). In these applications, the principle of dilution of material finds its utmost expression in a hierarchy of discretised members. The primary members are themselves

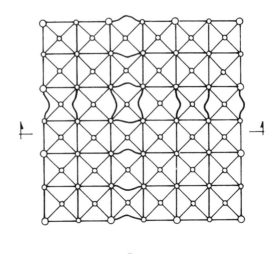

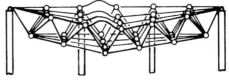

Typical DLG buckling pattern

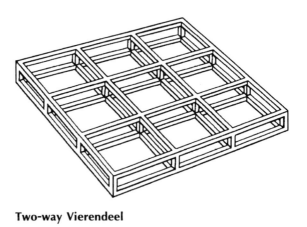

Two-way Vierendeel

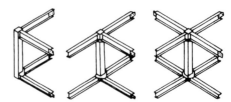

Components of the CUBIC system

discretised into secondary members. For instance the primary member may be a spatial truss.

Several ideas have been proposed for geometries of such grids, by joining together reticulated *polyhedra* (see next chapter – 11.7.2.2), the so called **Polyhedral lattices** or **Polyhedral networks**, but the concept has not found wide ranging acceptance to date.

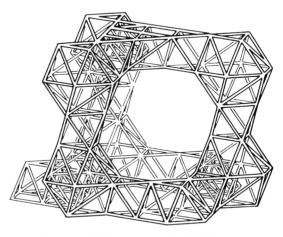

Modular unit of infinite polyhedral lattice (after M. Burt[2])

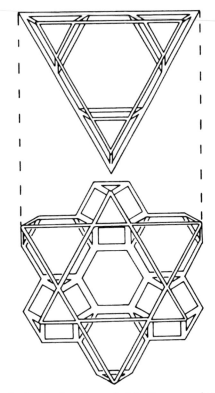

Polyhedral units forming a habitable space lattice (after J.F. Gabriel[3])

Geometry	Action mode	
	Direct	**Flexure**
Discrete		
Continuous		

11 Shells

Shells were presented in Chapter 10, at the geometric level, as a three-dimensional extension to arches of funicular shape. This is a limited viewpoint which is useful in the description of certain classes of shells (e.g. domes). In fact the term *Shell* applies to any curved surface in **membrane action**, namely capable of supporting loads through compression, tension and shear stresses within the surface. This definition implies a structural depth beyond the thickness of the shell.

11.1 Surface curvature

Different types of surface curvature are distinguished. The type of curvature can be tested by 'touching' a plane to the surface, so that the plane is **tangent** to the surface. The curvature is characterised by the relation of the tangent plane to the surface.

11.1.1 Single curvature

If the plane touches the surface along a straight line, the surface is said to possess a *Single curvature*. If we 'cut' the surface by a plane perpendicular to the line of 'touch', we obtain a curved cross-section. Singly curved surfaces are *Developable surfaces* – they can be produced from a planar surface (e.g. a sheet of paper).

11.1.2 Double curvature

If the tangent plane touches the surface at a point, the surface has *Double curvature*. There are at least two mutually orthogonal planes, which are perpendicular to the tangent plane and which pass through the tangent point, intersecting the surface along curves. Doubly curved surfaces are not developable. There are two types of doubly curved surfaces discussed in the following sections.

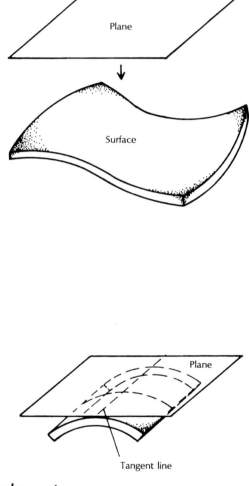

Single curvature

11.1.2.1 If the relation between the tangent plane and the surface is such that the surface, in the vicinity of the tangent point, lies completely to one side of the plane, the surface (or curvature) is said to be *Synclastic* in this vicinity. The surface as a whole is synclastic if it is synclastic at every point. In common parlance we can call it 'convex' or 'concave' (agreeing we look from the top, say).

11.1.2.2 If the surface is partly to one side of the tangent plane and partly to the other, the surface is said to be *Anticlastic* in the vicinity of the tangent point. The intersection curves of the surface with two orthogonal planes, perpendicular to the tangent plane through the tangent point, lie in different sides of the tangent plane (except for special orientations in which the two curves may be straight lines – see *hyperbolic paraboloid* in 11.5 below). In common parlance we may call it 'saddle shaped'.

> In mathematical terms, synclastic curves have positive **Gaussian curvature**, anticlastic curves have negative Gaussian curvature and singly curved surfaces have zero Gaussian curvature.

11.1.2.3 The surface of a shell may be composed of a combination of synclastic and anticlastic portions but if it incorporates planar portions these portions are, generally, subject to flexure.

11.2 Structural rings

Rings – closed convex curves – are often encountered in spatial structures either as boundary elements or in certain cross-sections. A *Ring*, in the structural sense, is a special type of funicular shape. It is a closed loop forming a funicular shape for a set of forces in equilibrium in the plane, in such a way that it is either in pure tension or in pure compression.

The rules for the shape of the funicular curve as a function of the load apply to rings. For example,

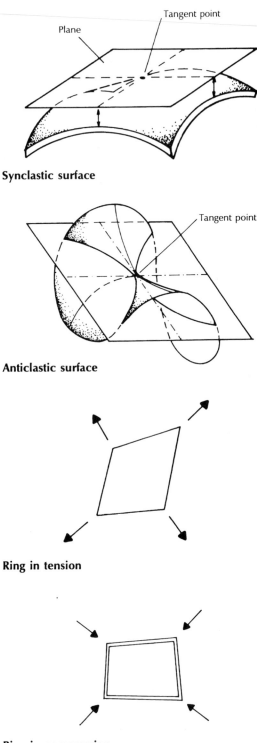

Synclastic surface

Anticlastic surface

Ring in tension

Ring in compression

the shape is a straight line for unloaded portions and a curved line for portions with distributed load. The shape is the shape a string would take under the applied loads (in the case of a tension ring) or with the direction of loads reversed (in the case of a compression ring). The relation of the moment diagram of a simply supported beam to a ring applies to free-body diagrams of portions of the ring, with forces applied by the removed portion considered as 'reactions'. Indeed, an arch or a cable can be considered as a portion of a ring.

Not every set of forces in equilibrium has a ring as its funicular shape. A ring as a pin-jointed planar structure is generally unstable (7.5.1). For equilibrium to be maintained, the relative position, orientation and magnitude of the forces have to be such that, at each vertex, the ring forces can balance the applied load.

11.3 Dome

A *Dome* is a structure of doubly curved surface (a shell, usually of convex curvature) covering an area of roughly regular shape (circular, polygonal).

The most prevalent type of dome since ancient times is the **Spherical dome**, whose surface is a segment of a sphere.

It is shown in the analysis that follows that a convex, doubly-curved surface, like the sphere, can support **any load** in membrane action, with the exception of point loads which cause some local bending. Unlike a funicular shape, therefore, the shape of a curved surface in direct action is not related to the load.

Some flexure may, and often does, arise along the boundary where support conditions may not be compatible with membrane action for a given load. Edge stiffening is normally required along boundaries to deal with this flexure.

The structural depth of domes is the full height of the dome, from base to crown. Depth to span ratios range from as low as $\frac{1}{8}$ for shallow domes to

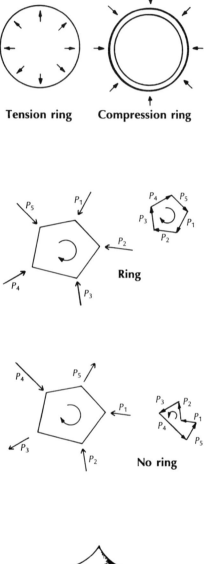

Tension ring   Compression ring

Ring

No ring

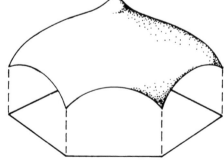

Dome

$\frac{1}{2}$ for deep domes. A depth/span ratio of $\frac{1}{5}$–$\frac{1}{4}$ is a common value which is near optimal for many applications. These values are characteristic of many other shell types as well.

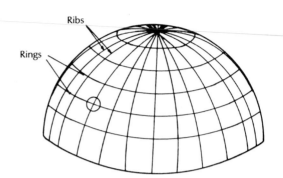

Spherical dome

11.3.1 Force analysis

In order to form an impression of the internal forces in a dome, let us inscribe on it a network of meridians – **ribs** – and latitudes – **rings**. Let us further assume that the loads on the dome are concentrated at the rib–ring joints and that the rings and ribs are straight lines between joints. As the spacing of ribs and rings decreases the approximation approaches the actual dome.

Let us consider the force equilibrium of a free-body diagram consisting of a joint and the connected bits of rib and ring, under a vertical load (due to the weight of the dome, for instance).

11.3.1.1 First, let us look at a vertical projection showing equilibrium of the rib. The external force (V) and the compression force in the rib above the joint (C_1), which is exerted by the part of the dome above the considered level, are balanced by the compression in the lower branch of the rib (C_2) and by a horizontal force H in the plane of the ring. This is the force exerted **by the ring on the rib**.

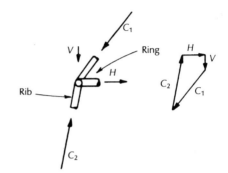

Vertical projection (rib)

11.3.1.2 Next let us look at a horizontal projection, showing the ring equilibrium. We see that the force H, when applied to the ring (in the opposite sense, since it is now the force exerted **by the rib on the ring**), is balanced by the force in the ring (tension or compression depending on the sense of H).

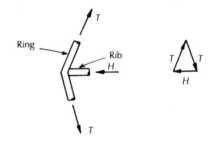

Horizontal projection (ring)

11.3.1.3 If we now look at a whole ring, acted upon by the horizontal components of all joints along that ring, we see that, under certain conditions, the ring can be the funicular shape of the

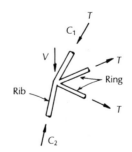

Three-dimensional view

forces and support them in compression or tension, depending on the sense of the forces.

For instance, if the rings are circular (as in a spherical dome), it would be the funicular shape for any axi-symmetric load, such as self weight or uniformly distributed load on a horizontal projection (all the radial components H being equal).

11.3.1.4 If the load is such that the ring is not a funicular shape for the horizontal components, part of the horizontal forces would be balanced by membrane shear forces, or diagonal normal forces (see note on principal axes in 10.1.1).

> This analysis demonstrates the fact that a doubly curved, pin-jointed, reticulated surface is stable only if the mesh is triangulated (see 11.6.2 below).

11.3.2 Forces in a spherical dome

In a spherical dome under symmetric load, the ring forces change from compression at the top to tension at the bottom (except for shallow domes). This tension caused a lot of trouble in historical domes, which were made of stone and incapable of sustaining tension.

If the shape of the ribs (meridian cross-sections) is the funicular shape for the load, then the forces in the rings vanish because full equilibrium is maintained by the ribs alone. This still leaves the problem of horizontal forces at the supports (see ring beam below).

11.3.3 Ring beam

Domes are often supported on vertical walls or columns. Whenever the direction of the support differs from the tangent to the ribs there is a special ring at the level of the support with concentration of tensile or compressive force – the **Ring beam** or **Edge ring**.

This ring provides the horizontal reaction resulting from the change in the direction of the

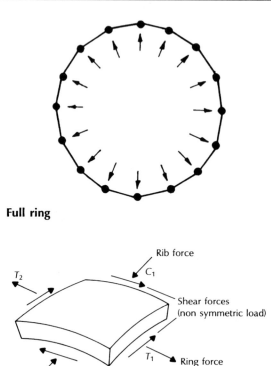

Full ring

Dome element

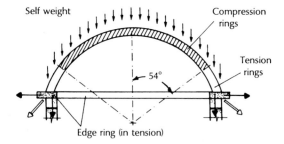

rib forces, from the tangent to the dome surface to the vertical. Whether the forces in the ring are tensile or compressive depends only on the sense of the change in direction. If the support rotates inward from the tangent (as is most common), the force in the ring beam is tensile. It does not depend on forces in adjacent interior rings. If the dome is supported on columns, the edge ring may be subjected to some bending.

It thus becomes evident that it is not possible to escape from some tension in domes supported on vertical columns or walls, since the funicular shape for the load (predominantly the weight of the dome) never has a vertical tangent. The obvious solution is inclined columns or walls, but this solution appears to have eluded the ancient dome builders.

11.3.4 Conical dome

Domes may be of various shapes other than spherical. A *Conical dome*, for instance, is of interest. It is singly curved and yet it works in direct (membrane) action similar to doubly curved domes, except that the ring forces do not change sense. They are always compressive for 'top-up' cones and tensile for 'top-down' cones (assuming support at the bottom). Some other dome shapes are encountered further down.

11.4 Shell geometries

Shell geometries can be generated in many and varied ways. For instance, a curved surface can be generated by moving one curve along another curve, or along a pair of curves. A very large repertory of shapes can be generated in this way, but certain classes of shell geometries are identified below.

When the 'fixed' curve – the **Generatrix** – is a horizontal curve, and the 'moving' curve – the **Generant** – is in a vertical plane, it is customary to

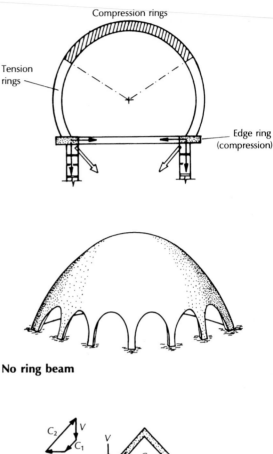

No ring beam

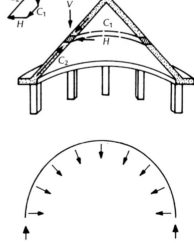

Conical dome

denote the surface with the generant as the name (the noun) and the generatrix as the attribute (the adjective). An example is *Hyperbolic paraboloid* – a vertical parabola moving along a horizontal hyperbola. It is often more convenient to visualise the surface in a different way (see following descriptions), so that the mathematical appellation seems sometimes obscure or confusing.

Shell surface generation

11.4.1 Cylindrical shells

Cylindrical shells can be generated by moving a curve, parallel to itself, along a straight line – or vice versa, moving the straight line along the curve. The latter generation clearly demonstrates that it is a surface of single curvature.

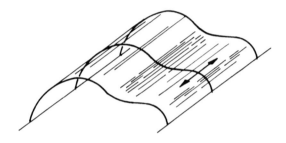

Cylindrical shell generation

11.4.1.1 Cylindrical shells are often used in one-way spanning structures, similar to folded plates (10.4). In fact, a folded plate can be regarded, from the geometric viewpoint, as a cylindrical shell with the 'curve' consisting of straight lines (a polygon). From the structural viewpoint there is a difference in that the shell acts primarily in membrane action whereas the folded plate acts also in bending.

Like folded plates, such cylindrical shells require stiff gable walls for their supports to maintain their shape and ensure membrane action. Free edges require stiffening to prevent local buckling and bending.

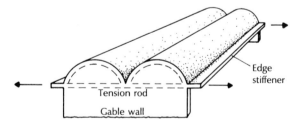

Cylindrical shell

11.4.1.2 The difference between cylindrical shell and barrel vault. A cylindrical shell may have a shape similar to a barrel vault (9.7), but the structural action is completely different. A barrel vault is a **planar** structure, having the **funicular shape** spanning across the **curved** cross-section – the **width**. It requires continuous or closely spaced supports along the edges, but the gable ends may remain open.

A cylindrical shell, by contrast, spans along its **length** (along the straight line direction); its edges may remain without any supports, but the gable ends must be stiff (in their plane).

A barrel vault transmits horizontal forces to the supports along its entire length, under vertical loads. In a cylindrical shell the horizontal thrust is concentrated in the gable walls, and it is often resisted by a tension rod in the wall.

A barrel vault sustains bending under any but the load for which it is the funicular shape. A cylindrical shell acts in direct membrane action under most loads. Point loads are an exception.

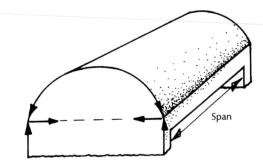

Cylindrical shell

11.4.2 Conoidal shell

A *Conoidal shell* or *Conoid* is produced when a straight line is slid along a curve at one end and a straight line at the other end. The resulting surface is generally doubly curved.

11.4.2.1 Conoidal shells are normally used as spanning structures, similar to cylindrical shells. They are particularly effective for cantilever configuration, because the structural depth varies from near zero at one end – the free end – to a maximum at the other end – the fixed end – where the overall bending moment is maximum.

Barrel vault

It should be noted that the fixed end – the gable wall for instance – should be able to support the bending moment and therefore should have lateral as well as in-plane stiffness. To achieve this the vertical supports can also be shells – cylindrical or conoidal – which form a **shell frame** with the horizontal part, similar to a folded frame (10.4.3).

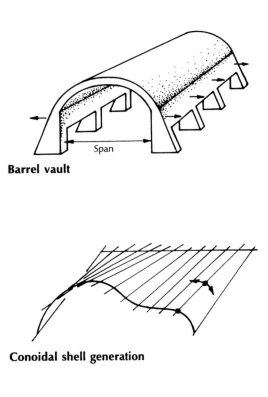

Conoidal shell generation

11.4.3 Ruled surface

A *Ruled surface* is produced by sliding a straight line over a pair of curves. Cylindrical and conoidal shells are particular cases of ruled surfaces. Ruled surfaces may be singly or doubly curved (see, for instance, *hyperbolic paraboloid* below).

Conoidal shell as cantilever

11.4.4 Shells of revolution

Shells of revolution are produced by rotating a curve around a circle. Spherical and conical domes are examples of shells of revolution, but any curve can be used.

11.4.5 Translational shells

Translational shells are produced by translating a curve (moving in a parallel fashion) over another curve. Cylindrical shells can be seen as translational shells, the generatrix being a straight line. This is a useful technique for generating domes over rectangular areas.

Example

We want to cover a square area with a dome. We could use a spherical dome and **Truncate** it (i.e. cut and remove the cut parts) by vertical planes at the perimeter walls, obtaining circular arches along the boundaries.

We could obtain a similar result using a **Translational dome**. Translating a circular arc over an identical arc perpendicular to it would generate a dome very similar to the truncated spherical dome. If the domes are relatively shallow, it would be difficult to tell them apart.

> The difference can be seen in the boundary arches. In the truncated sphere the radius of the arches is smaller than that of the dome. In vertical projection the two are concentric. In the translational dome the radius of the arches is identical to the radius at any vertical plane parallel to the boundary. The translational surface is not spherical.

11.4.6 Soap film shells

As the name implies, a **Soap film shell** over a given boundary has the shape a soap film would acquire when a wire frame model of the boundary is

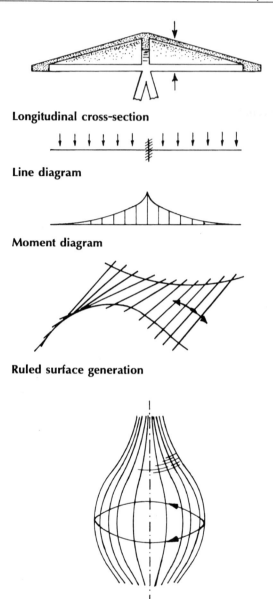

Longitudinal cross-section

Line diagram

Moment diagram

Ruled surface generation

Shell of revolution

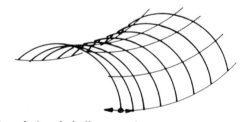

Translational shell generation

soaked in soap solution, scaled appropriately. Soap film surfaces are sometimes referred to as **Minimal surfaces**, having the property of minimum surface area for a given boundary. They also have the property of constant tension, that is, the tension in any direction of any shell element is constant. Soap bubble models can be a useful tool in shell design, particularly for complex boundaries. Soap film surfaces can also be computer simulated, with the added advantage that the surface can be modified to accommodate functional and other constraints.

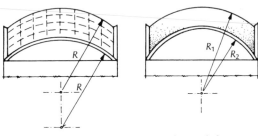

Translational dome   Spherical dome

11.4.7 Free-form shells

Free-form shells are shell surfaces which are not readily expressed as mathematical functions. They can be formed by various means, such as physical models. Free-form shells can be computer generated by using optimisation techniques and prescribing various constraints such as boundary layout, points of support, prescribed heights at selected points, conditions on membrane and other forces etc.

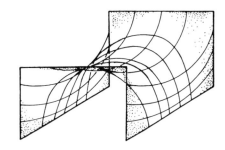

Soap-film (minimal) surface

Free-form shell

11.4.8 Sponge shells

Sponge shells or **Sponge lattices** are space filling anticlastic surfaces. These are continuous structures similar to the space filling polyhedral lattices (10.8.2) which are discrete structures. The spaces in the network can be used for functional purposes. Few, if any, large-scale structures of this type have been constructed, although many conceptual ideas have been proposed.

11.5 Hyperbolic paraboloid

A **Hyperbolic paraboloid** (HYPAR) is a ubiquitous shell, owing to its geometric properties which

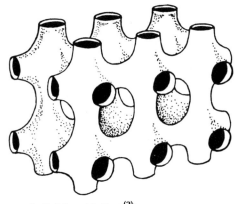

Sponge shell (after M. Burt[2])

make it convenient for execution in concrete. The simplest way to define it geometrically is as a ruled surface produced by sliding a straight line over two non coplanar straight lines.

A simple way to visualize (and to construct) the surface is to draw a square (or rectangle) on a horizontal plane and then lift one corner of the rectangle, leaving all edges straight. The HYPAR is a surface bounded by this 'skew rectangle', having the properties listed below.

11.5.1 Geometric properties of the HYPAR

❑ Any line 'parallel' to the boundary (i.e. obtained by the intersection of a vertical plane parallel to the boundary with the surface) is straight.
❑ This is the main reason for the popularity of this surface – it contains two orthogonal families of straight lines making it convenient for forming by wood planks. Curved formwork is a major contributor to the cost of shell construction. Another reason for their popularity is the rectangular plan which is convenient for covering rectangular areas.
❑ The surface is **anticlastic** (saddle-shaped). A vertical plane along the diagonal connecting the two opposite 'low' corners intersects the surface along a convex parabola. The other diagonal produces a concave parabola (looking from the 'top') – hence the 'paraboloid' in the name.
❑ Horizontal planes intersect the surface along hyperbolas, with the lower boundaries as asymptotes (i.e. the boundaries connecting the three vertices in the horizontal plane), hence the first part of the name.
❑ If we rotate the surface somewhat around the two opposing 'low' corners we can get a symmetric HYPAR with two opposing 'high' corners.

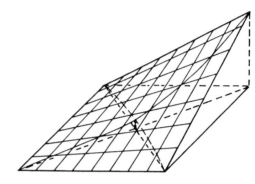

Hyperbolic paraboloid (HYPAR)

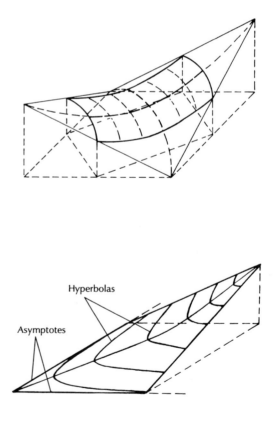

Hyperbolas

Asymptotes

- The saddle shape appears clearly if we truncate the surface of this symmetric HYPAR by vertical planes, parallel to the diagonals. The new boundaries are alternating convex and concave parabolas.
- HYPARs can be combined in a variety of ways to produce complex surfaces, including sponge lattices. Very efficient configurations can be produced, from the structural viewpoint (see below).

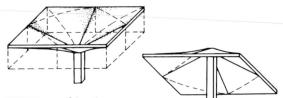

HYPAR combinations

11.5.2 'Flow' of forces in a HYPAR

11.5.2.1 Internal forces can be analysed quite simply in the HYPAR under uniformly distributed load. The parabolas in the surface form two orthogonal families. One family consists of convex parabolas, namely arches (in compression). The other family consists of concave parabolas, namely cables (in tension). There are no shear forces under uniformly distributed load in directions parallel to the diagonals. These directions are the **principal axes** (10.1.1).

11.5.2.2 At the boundary the tensile force of a 'cable' meets the compressive force of an 'arch'. The resultant force is directed along the *Boundary member*. **Provided the HYPAR is properly supported, the boundary member acts axially** (in tension or compression). The member is in tension if it is supported at its 'tail' (tail end of the force vector) and in compression if supported at its 'head'. 'Supported' implies restrained in the axial direction. If it is supported at both ends it is subject to tension in the vicinity of the 'tail' and to compression in the vicinity of the 'head'.

11.5.2.3 The trick in 'proper support' is to ensure that at least one end of each boundary member is restrained both vertically and horizontally. The horizontal components are usually the main problem. The optimal way is to design HYPAR

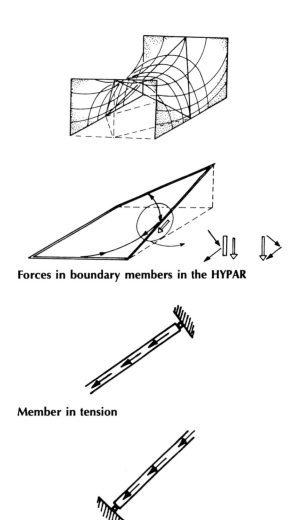

Forces in boundary members in the HYPAR

Member in tension

Member in compression

combinations in which horizontal components of adjacent units 'cancel out', leaving only vertical resultants which can be picked up by columns.

Columns should be placed at intersection points of sloping boundary members. The number of required columns can be minimised by placing them at points, where the maximum number of sloping boundary members intersect, since it is sufficient to support a sloping member at one end only.

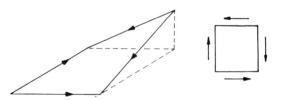

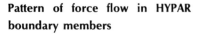

Pattern of force flow in HYPAR boundary members

The direction of flow of boundary forces can be obtained by the analysis outlined above. However, there is a very simple rule which makes it very easy to follow force flow in boundary members, and to design the supports properly: **the forces flow like water** – from a high point to a low point.

It is enough to determine the direction of flow in one member. The rest follow (from equilibrium) in a similar pattern to shear forces (10.1.1) – into the corner or away from the corner.

11.5.2.4 It should be noted that the structural depth of the HYPAR, or of any saddle-shaped (anticlastic) shell, is, for each of the families of convex and concave curves, its own rise or sag, and not the overall depth of the structure. In general, the structural depth is approximately $\frac{1}{2}$ the total height. When several HYPARs are used in conjunction, the structural depth of the structure as a whole may be the full depth of the structure, provided it is 'properly supported'. A minimum structural depth of approximately $\frac{1}{10}$ of the span should be maintained for efficient performance.

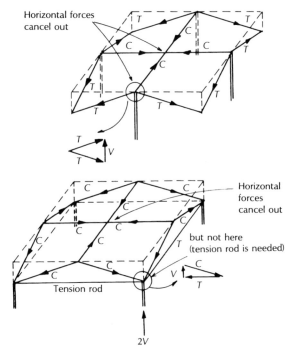

Effect of support conditions on boundary member forces

11.6 Plate shells and braced shells

11.6.1 Plate shells

In 10.3 and 10.4 the concept of a hinged plate element was introduced as a three-dimensional extension to a pin-ended bar element. The concept of a pin-jointed bar network was similarly extended to a hinge-jointed plate network. The

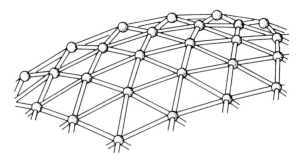

Pin-jointed braced shell

smooth surface of any shell can be substituted by
either a pin-jointed bar network, forming a
Braced shell, or a hinge-jointed plate network,
forming a **Plate shell**.

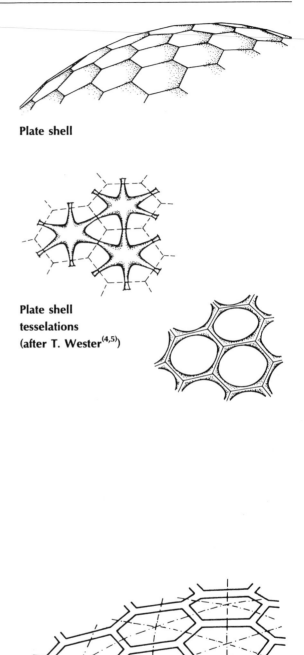

Plate shell

A **Plate network** is to a large extent a theoretical
concept. It consists of planar surfaces bounded
by polygonal edges. If the plates are complete,
i.e. have no holes in them, then the network is
automatically a combination of hinged plate and
pinned bar network, since the edges forming the
plate hinges also serve as bars, and the intersection of these hinged edges – the vertices of the
polyhedral surface – form pin joints. However,
since plates do not require vertices but only
edges along their hinged boundaries, these vertices
could be removed to produce 'holes'. If these holes
are enlarged, a reticulated structure is obtained.
A different reticulation can be obtained by cutting
the holes around the centres of the plates.

**Plate shell
tesselations
(after T. Wester[4,5])**

11.6.2 Rigidity and mode of action

11.6.2.1 For a curved pin-jointed bar network to
be geometrically rigid, it has, in general, to consist
of triangles. Any rigid-jointed bar network is
geometrically rigid, but the members may be
subject to flexure, as well as to axial forces.

The condition for rigidity of a pure hinged plate
network is that its vertices are three valenced, i.e.
that three edges intersect at a vertex. This is
because if the vertex joint is removed, that is a
hole is formed round the vertex, the shape of the
hole should be triangular for the system to be rigid.
Any other polygon would be unstable.

The difference between a pin-jointed bar network and a reticulated hinged plate network should
not be underestimated. Both are subject to direct
action. However, while the bars in a pin-jointed
network are subject to **axial** action, the members of
the plate network are part of a plate and are
subject to **membrane** action, which includes shear
forces in the plane of the plate. As the 'holes' in the

Rigid-jointed braced shell

plate are made large, leaving only narrow strips of material, the shear forces cause **bending** of these strips, in the plane of the plate. As a result, the 'bar-like' strips of a plate network would generally have a larger cross-section than bars in pin-jointed networks.

The concept of hinged plate network is subtle and more difficult to comprehend than that of a bar network, but the relation between the two is fundamental. The plate network can be termed the 'dual' of the bar network in the geometrical, as well as structural, sense. It is interesting to note that polyhedra consisting of triangles (see comment in 11.7.2.2 below) are rigid as pin-jointed bar networks, but not as plate networks, whereas their geometric duals are stable as plate networks but not as pin-jointed bar networks. (The dual of a polyhedron is obtained by substituting a vertex with a face and vice versa. Thus, the cube is the dual of the octahedron, the dodecahedron is the dual of the icosahedron and the tetrahedron is its own dual.)

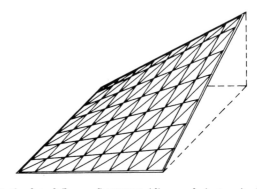

Reticulated (braced) HYPAR (diagonals in tension)

11.6.2.2 Braced shells made of steel bars are very thin compared with concrete shells. The primary mode of failure is buckling in various forms – member buckling, local (snap-through) buckling and general buckling.

When spans are large the curvature is often very low. Due to length tolerances (inaccuracies in member lengths), areas with very small or vanishing curvatures can result, leading to local instability. Double-layer grid configurations are often used in shells of large spans in order to stiffen the shell. Note, however, that structural depth is still the total rise of the shell (from the supports) and not the grid depth as in DLGs of planar surface (10.7).

11.7 Braced domes

Braced domes are the most common form of large span domes built today. The large span is facilitated by the low weight (typically 40–$80\,\text{kg/m}^2$ total weight, including covering). There are many

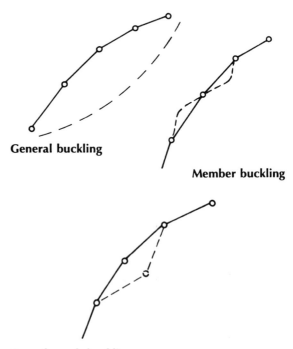

General buckling

Member buckling

Snap-through buckling

dome geometries, characterised by the pattern of discretisation of the surface. Three general classes can be identified, as described below.

11.7.1 Ribbed domes

In **Ribbed domes** the surface is divided into a network of meridional ribs and latitudinal rings, similar to the imaginary subdivision used for analytical purposes (11.3.1).

As indicated above, such a rectangular network is not geometrically rigid (and not stable) as a pin-jointed system, although equilibrium can be maintained under symmetrical loads.

The network can be stabilised in one of three ways:

(1) Diagonals are added to form a triangulated network. The diagonals serve in a secondary role for asymmetric loads.
(2) By employing rigid joints. In this case members are subject to bending moments under asymmetric loads.
(3) By the use of the roof sheeting as a diaphragm to rigidify the structure. The sheeting and its connections need to be designed for the shear forces arising from asymmetric loads.

11.7.2 Grid domes

In **Grid domes** the surface is covered by a pin-jointed triangular grid, or by a rigid jointed, non triangular, surface-filling grid (e.g. hexagonal) or by a tessellated (patterned) plate network.

It should be noted that **a triangular grid of convex surface cannot be regular**, i.e. it is not possible to cover a non developable surface with equilateral triangles (since six equilateral triangles form a 360° angle at their joint, which defines a plane).

11.7.2.1 In a relatively shallow dome (rise to span ratio of $\frac{1}{6}$ or less) it is practical to obtain the grid by projecting a planar grid (triangular, for instance) onto the dome surface. Because of the

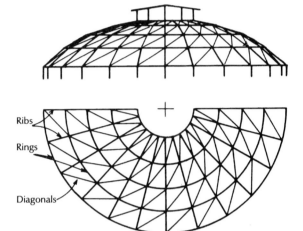

Ribbed dome

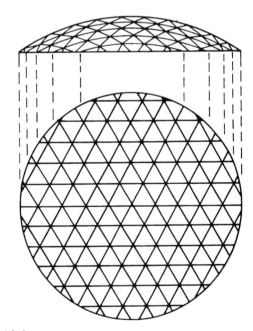

Grid dome

curvature, the triangles (or other polygons) are distorted, so that they are more nearly regular at the top and more distorted near the perimeter. The distortion is larger the larger the curvature of the dome (i.e. the rise). The density of bars around the perimeter is lower than near the top, and the bars are longer. This is undesirable, since forces are larger near the perimeter than at the top.

A more favourable division, particularly for deeper domes, may be obtained by **Geodesic projection** of the planar grid onto the curved surface. The planar grid nodes are projected by radii from the centre of the enveloping sphere. Improved regularity can be achieved by various techniques of geodesic projection (see *geodesic dome* below).

The term 'geodesic' in this context refers to the fact that every edge of the grid thus projected forms part of a **great circle** of the enveloping sphere, or a geodesic.

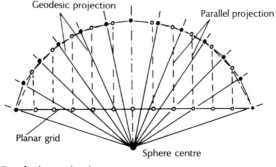

Geodesic projection

11.7.2.2 *Geodesic dome*

The term and concept were formulated by R. Buckminster Fuller (although earlier examples are known). This is a grid dome suitable for deep domes (domes with high rise to span ratio, typically larger than about $\frac{1}{5}$).

The objective of the idea is to minimise the distortions of the triangular network and maximise its regularity. The method of realising this objective is to start not with a planar grid but with a **Regular polyhedron** (see note on polyhedra below).

A polyhedron is a closed surface consisting of planar facets (*poly* – many, *hedron* – facet, in Greek). In a regular polyhedron the facets are all identical regular polygons (equilateral triangles, squares or pentagons).

The geodesic dome grid is obtained by subdividing each face of the polyhedron into a triangular grid and geodesically projecting this grid onto the dome surface.

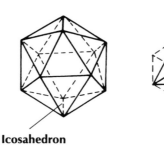

Icosahedron

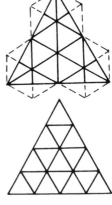

Subdivision patterns

The most popular polyhedron for generation of geodesic domes is the *Icosahedron*, which has 20 equilateral triangular facets. The reason for its popularity is that, of the five regular polyhedra, it is the polyhedron with the largest number of facets and these facets are triangles.

The number of different triangles (or different bar lengths) depends on the *Frequency of subdivision* – the number of segments into which each edge of the polyhedron face is divided.

Since the dome forms only part of the polyhedron, the polyhedron has to be 'trimmed', often producing some irregular configurations near the edge which do not fit into the general pattern.

Regular polyhedra: there are only five regular polyhedra (the so called Platonian polyhedra) – the tetrahedron, with 4 equilateral triangular faces; the cube or hexahedron, with 6 square faces; the octahedron, with 8 triangular faces; the dodecahedron, with 12 pentagonal faces; and the icosahedron, with 20 triangular faces.

Polyhedra with triangular (and/or hexagonal) faces are most suitable for generation of triangular grids. The squares and pentagons do not divide into triangles in a regular fashion.

A large number of **semi regular** polyhedra (the so called Archimedean polyhedra) can be produced from the regular ones by processes of truncation (cutting and removing vertices), snubbing (adding vertices) and duality (interchanging faces and vertices).

These polyhedra consist of non identical faces but all edges are of equal length. Some of these polyhedra are suitable for triangular mesh generation.

The original polyhedron in a geodesic dome can be detected by the presence of some unique vertices. While in most vertices six triangles (or members) join, in vertices corresponding to vertices of the original polyhedron there are fewer triangles – five for an icosahedron, four for an octahedron and three for a tetrahedron.

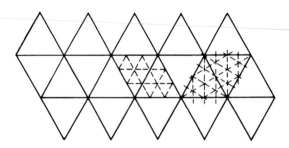

Unfolded pattern of icosahedron (with subdivision patterns)

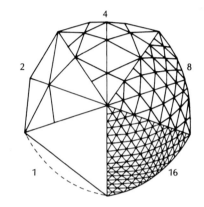

Subdivision frequencies

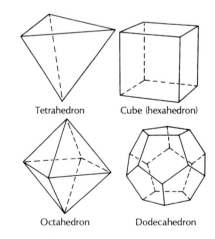

Tetrahedron   Cube (hexahedron)

Octahedron   Dodecahedron

Regular (Platonian) polyhedra

11.7.3 Lamella domes

The basic unit of a **Lamella dome** is a diamond-shaped cell. The term 'lamella' refers to the technique of construction rather than the grid pattern.

The joints in the grid are in fact 'half joints' – two member ends join at the middle of a crossing member. The length of each member is twice the length of a unit cell.

Rigidity of the surface is often achieved by rigid jointing of the members. Alternatively, the surface may be stiffened either by adding diagonal members along the short diagonals of the rhombi or by employing the roof covering as a stiffening diaphragm.

Many patterns of surface subdivision are possible. The main merit of this type of grid is the simplicity of the joints. It is often employed in timber domes. The joining members can be offset to enable separate joining of each member.

The members are usually deep relative to their width, giving the surface high flexural stiffness and enabling large spans without the need for double-layer arrangements, which complicate the joints considerably.

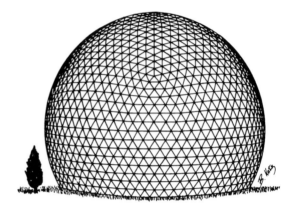

Expo 67, Montréal

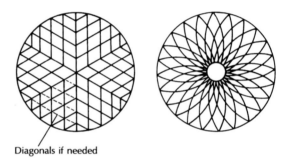

Diagonals if needed

Lamella dome patterns

Lamella pattern

Possible connection

Geometry	Action mode	
	Direct	**Flexure**
Discrete		 **Secondary action**
Continuous		**None**

12 Tension Structures

12.1 Extension of the cable concept

The extension of the cable concept to spatial geometries is not as straightforward as the extension
of the arch concept to shells due to the deformability and the need for prestress (8.3, 9.1.1.2).

Tension spatial structures (*cable nets* and *fabric
structures*) are normally employed for the covering of areas. They are the lightest structures
known (per unit surface) and therefore they are
subject to load reversal under wind. Since the
surface has no flexural stiffness it cannot sustain
compression forces.

In order to support alternating loads, **the
surface of a tension structure must be prestressed**
(in tension), so that the resultant forces in it
(under prestress and the load) are always tensile.

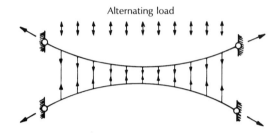

Planar prestressed cable system

12.1.1 Tensioned surface geometry

12.1.1.1 The way to prestress a curved cable in
the plane is to connect it, by means of ties, with
another cable of opposite curvature. Pulling one
of the cables automatically induces tension in
both cables. Any load applied to the structure
increases the tension in one of the cables and
reduces the tension in the other. Although the
structure is deformable, deflections are within
acceptable limits for this type of structure.
Deflections can be controlled by controlling the
prestress force in the cables.

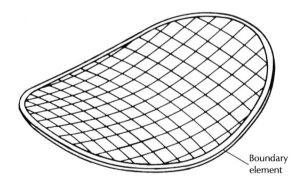

Spatial prestressed cable net

12.1.1.2 The extension of this concept to spatial
structures is a **Cable net**. The two cables are
replaced by two orthogonal families of cables with
opposing curvatures. The result is an **anticlastic
(saddle-shaped) surface** (surface of negative Gaus-
sian curvature). Inducing tension in one family

automatically introduces tension in the other. There is no need for ties.

A cable net can be defined as a pretensioned pin-jointed orthogonal network having an anticlastic surface.

12.1.1.3 If the surface is made of continuous material – usually fabric – the structure is termed *Fabric structure* or *Tensioned membrane*. A fabric structure is a pretensioned anticlastic surface.

> Fabric structures are sometimes termed **membrane structures**, which perhaps better describes their physical nature since they need not be actually made of fabric. However, this terminology causes confusion with the definition of membrane action, which allows compression.

12.1.2 Structural properties

The properties of cable nets and fabric structures are reviewed together, because the geometries and the major features and requirements are similar.

12.1.2.1 Cable networks usually consist of quadrilateral cells – they are formed of cables in two approximately orthogonal directions. There is no need for triangulation of the surface, since the structure is geometrically deformable in the vertical direction, so there is no significant benefit in rigidifying the surface.

The main difference between cable nets and fabric structures, from the structural viewpoint, is that fabric structures are capable of sustaining membrane shear forces whereas cable nets are not, due to the deformability of the surface.

The cables are initially laid in the principal directions of the prestress (the cables automatically assume this position). More accurately, the prestress forces are designed to fit the desired layout of the cables and the surface geometry. Cable orientation varies somewhat under different loads, as the forces in them change, but provided

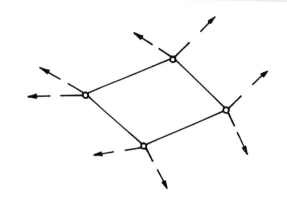

Forces in cable net

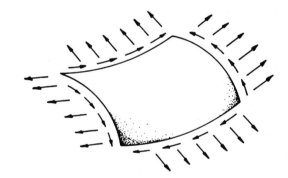

Forces in tensioned membrane

the prestress forces are large enough, these deformations are not excessive.

12.1.2.2 Fabric structures are capable of developing limited shear forces (depending on the nature of the fabric). The strength and stiffness (elastic modulus) of fabrics is considerably lower than that of steel cables. For this reason fabric and cables are often used in conjunction, with cables serving as stiffening elements. In any case, cable net roofs usually employ fabric as covering, so it makes structural sense (although it is not always economical) to combine the two materials in a **composite** mode of action.

Soap film surfaces are particularly suitable for fabric structures as they ensure uniform tension throughout. Some fabrics are orthotropic, that is they have different properties (e.g. strength) in two orthogonal directions. Computer modelling enables soap film geometries to be modified in order to accommodate different tension in the two directions.

12.1.2.3 One of the main problems in fabric structure design is the establishment of *Cutting patterns*. Since the doubly curved surface is not developable, that is it cannot be shaped out of a flat piece of fabric, it has to be produced by joining together several pieces of fabric. The goal is to shape the pieces so that when the membrane is tensioned it assumes the correct shape, without forming ripples. Ripples are an indication that compressive forces tend to develop in the surface (in the direction perpendicular to the ripples). The cutting patterns should also ensure that the fabric is oriented so that the fibres in it (the weft and warp) are oriented, as closely as practicable, in the principal directions at every point.

12.2 Boundary elements and anchorage

Purely tensile structures do not exist. There must always be elements in compression, otherwise

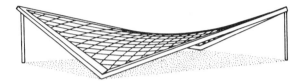

Fabric structure

Cutting pattern of a typical strip

equilibrium cannot be maintained. The compressed elements may be in the ground, or even the ground itself, but a closed prestressed system must include both tensile and compressive stresses. The tensioned cables or fabric must be **anchored** against some rigid element or elements at their boundary.

The anchoring element can take various forms. It may be a rigid structural element such as a beam, an arch or other elements in compression or flexure. It may be a whole rigid network such as a truss (planar or spatial), frame etc. In the latter case the structure consists, in effect, of two classes of substructures – a rigid bar structure and a deformable tension structure. Such structures are termed *Hybrid structures*.

The boundary elements are an important part of the tension structure as they determine the shape and nature of not just the boundary but the surface as a whole (see, for instance soap film surfaces, 11.4.6).

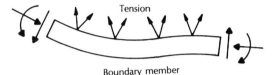

Tension

Boundary member

12.2.1 Straight (flexural) boundary elements

When the boundary elements are straight members, they generally act in flexure.

The HYPAR (11.5) is a prestressable surface (anticlastic) with straight boundary elements. It was shown that under uniformly distributed load and with proper support, the boundary members act axially. Under uniformly distributed load, one family of parabolas forming the surface is in tension and the other is in compression. The resultant force is oriented along the boundary member.

Under prestress, however, both sets of parabolas are in tension and the resultant is directed perpendicular to the boundary member which then acts in flexure (irrespective of the method of support). Naturally, the boundary element can be made as a truss, rather than a beam or a frame. In this case the truss members are subject to direct action (compression and tension).

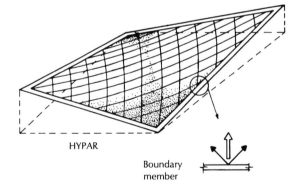

HYPAR

Boundary member

Many prestressable geometries can be generated with straight boundary elements, including various combinations of HYPARs and soap film surfaces.

12.2.2 *Compression boundary elements*

12.2.2.1 An arch is an extremely efficient boundary element for tension structures. Provided the prestress introduces no bending in the arch, it is practically impossible for the arch to buckle under the prestress load. No bending in the arch implies that the arch is the funicular shape for the prestress forces and it is properly anchored to the ground, or to other parts of the structure, so that the resultant prestress forces are in the plane and axis of the arch.

Sideways buckling is restrained by the cables, fabric or anchorage elements crossing the arch. Any buckling in the plane of the arch involves the extension of some of the cross-cables, which tend to pull it back into position. The bicycle wheel is an ideal example of this principle (see below).

Arches can be used as intermediate boundary elements in multiple surface arrangements, allowing for the covering of large areas. Arches of large spans are often made as trusses.

12.2.2.2 *Posts* are often used as support and anchorage elements in tension structures (e.g. tents). They are not, strictly speaking, boundary elements, because they do not form part of the surface or its boundary, but they serve as anchorage to cables which form part of the surface or the boundary (see *soft boundary* below).

Posts are usually long, laterally unbraced compression members, subject to high compressive forces. They are, therefore, subject to buckling under all loads (prestress as well as applied) and are often very bulky.

Posts cannot be used directly as anchorage in fabric structures due to the high concentration of

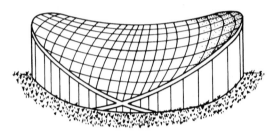

Arches as boundary elements

Concentrically
prestressed member

Prestressed arch

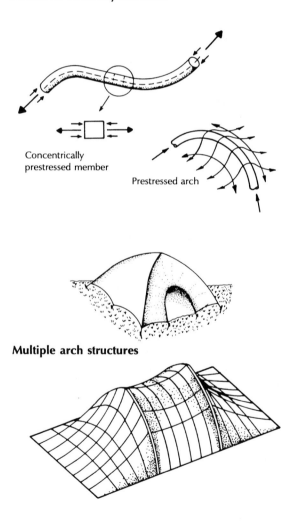

Multiple arch structures

stress at the tip. The forces have to be transferred to the post via a system of cables or rigid 'saddles'.

12.2.3 Tension boundary elements

Cables can be used as boundary elements. This is a geometrically deformable boundary, often termed **Soft boundary**. Due to their geometric deformability, they contribute to the deformability of the structure as a whole. It is difficult to ensure a precise prestressed geometry with soft boundaries. This is a problem with fabric structures in particular where it can lead to ripples in the surface, indicating zones where tension is not maintained in every direction.

Naturally, a cable as boundary element is not sufficient to anchor the structure as it needs anchorage itself, either in the ground directly or through some other compression element. Posts are often used in combination with soft boundaries (tent structures, Munich stadium).

12.2.4 Rings as boundary elements

Tension structures with circular or oval layouts may have rings as boundary elements. Usually such structures incorporate an outer compression ring and an inner tension ring. Since the rings are closed they do not require anchorage or support for the prestress forces. The structure as a whole can be supported either at the centre or at the perimeter.

As mentioned above, properly prestressed, the compression ring cannot buckle under the prestress load. It is relatively easy to prestress a circular ring 'properly', since a circle is the funicular shape of 'hydrostatic pressure', i.e. uniformly distributed **radial** force, so that all radial cables (or radial directions) need to be equally tensioned. The ring remains the funicular shape for any axi-symmetric load. Buckling is possible only under high asymmetric loads.

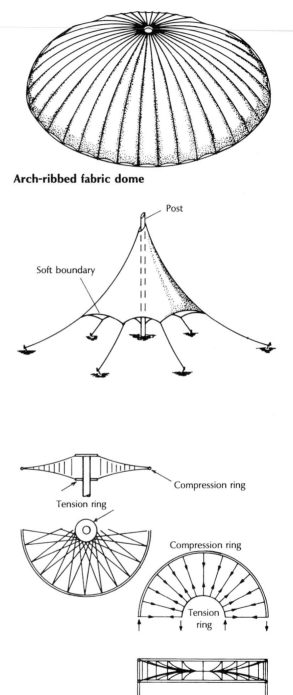

Arch-ribbed fabric dome

Rings as boundary elements

To achieve the anticlastic surface in a free standing structure, two layers of cables, or one layer of fabric and another of cables, are often required. The two layers are prestressed one against the other (see 12.1.1.1). Alternative arrangements are possible, such as outer ring and central post, with the ring anchored to the ground or to other structural elements, similar to a tent.

The bicycle wheel is an example of this type of structure. It is one of the most efficient structures known. It is generally loaded in its plane by most unfavourable loads – high concentrated loads, including impact – and yet it rarely buckles (when properly adjusted). For loads applied directly to the rings (the shaft and the rim), it is a rigid structure due to the straight tendons – the spokes. It can take high loads perpendicular to its plane as well.

12.3 Air-supported structures

Air-supported structures or *Pneumatic structures* (the terms are used interchangeably) are special kinds of fabric structures. They do not require an anticlastic surface for prestress. The tension is provided by air pressure.

The compression 'elements' are not concentrated at the boundary but are spread throughout the surface. The air itself is the main compression element. Additional compression elements may include boundary elements such as ring beams.

Two types of pneumatic structures are distinguished which are quite different in their way of action.

12.3.1 Ground anchored pneumatic structures

In these structures the air pressure applied to the tension surface is counteracted by the ground. Relatively low air pressure is continuously supplied into the space under the fabric. Special pressure traps are provided at entrances to maintain air 'tightness'.

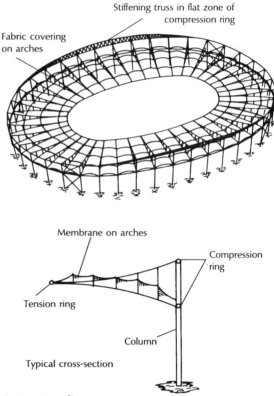

Stiffening truss in flat zone of compression ring

Fabric covering on arches

Membrane on arches

Compression ring

Tension ring

Column

Typical cross-section

Stuttgart stadium

Bicycle wheel

The air pressure just needs to balance the self weight of the membrane and the expected superimposed loads, such as snow or wind. These loads are usually relatively low – in the range of 0.2–1.0 kN/m^2 (0.03–0.14 psi), depending on geographic location.

It may appear as though pneumatic structures are 'pure' tensile structures (if the air is ignored). This impression is misleading, however, since the bulk of the structure lies under the ground. The total force of the air pressure has to be resisted by the **weight** of the foundations, or by deep ground anchors. In the latter case, the weight of the ground over the anchors serves as counterweight.

In addition to the membrane, external cables are usually added for improved anchorage and stiffness, and in order to limit membrane tension. Cables are sometimes employed to create special morphological effects.

These structures are very sensitive to non symmetric loads, since it is hard to balance such loads by the essentially uniform air pressure. A local load, such as snow drifts, in excess of the air pressure can create a dimple which may lead to collapse of the whole structure.

Power blackout and puncture and ripping of the membrane, causing loss of air pressure, are additional risks associated with this type of structure.

Two types are encountered and will be discussed in the following sections.

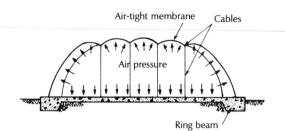

Air-supported (pneumatic) structure

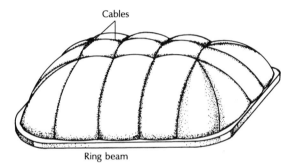

Deep profiled pneumatic structure

12.3.1.1 Deep profiled surfaces

These are anchored directly to the ground and require relatively low air pressure and low density (high spacing) of anchoring cables, due to the large structural depth. However, loss of pressure implies total collapse of the structure. Such collapse entails complete loss of the functional volume but, more importantly, a risk to potential occupants.

12.3.1.2 Shallow profiled surfaces

These serve as a roof to a rigid structure, typically a stadium, and are anchored not to the ground but to the structure via a ring beam.

This pneumatic structure requires higher pressure than deep profiled surfaces, because of the lower structural depth and the possibility of snow accumulation on flat surface. A higher density (close spacing) of external cables is also required to support the increased tension.

Loss of pressure causes 'inversion' of the surface, but the inverted roof does not fill the space underneath, resulting in a more benign form of failure than for ground anchored structures.

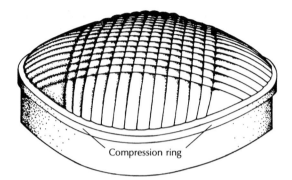

Shallow profile pneumatic roof

12.3.2 *High pressure pneumatic structures*

In these structures the membrane consists of a closed volume filled with high air pressure. This volume does not normally serve a functional purpose. A sealed 'tube' is the simplest example of such a structure (a rubber boat, for instance). A continuous air supply is not required, provided air tightness is ensured.

This is the nearest to a pure tension structure (if the enclosed air is ignored). No boundary members or anchoring are required for the prestress, but only for applied loads. A structure can be constructed by joining such tubes together or by using some rigid framing to shape the volume enclosed by the membrane (a 'pneumatic lens', for instance).

Structurally, this type of pneumatic structure is considerably less efficient than the ground anchored type. The low efficiency is due to the low structural depth, which is limited to the depth of the space enclosed by the membrane. Consequently, a very high air pressure is required to provide sufficient tension to counter any compression caused by the applied loads. Special and expensive materials have to be employed to sustain the high tension.

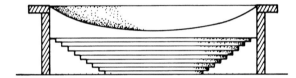

Deflated roof

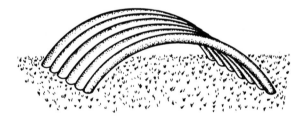

Double skinned, high pressure pneumatic structure, consisting of tubes

There are two main advantages to this system. (a) Once the closed space is pressurised it is sealed and there is no need for continuous pumping of air. (b) Since the closed system is in self equilibrium under air pressure, there is no need for substantial ground anchoring Due to the low structural efficiency, however, potential applications are limited. Deployable structures are an obvious application due to the ease of packaging, deployment (erection) and dismantling.

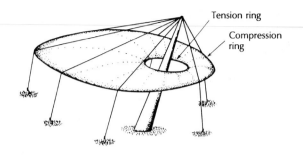

'Pneumatic lens'

12.4 Cable domes

The term *Cable dome* appears, at first glance, to be an oxymoron, since a cable is a structural component acting in tension whereas a dome is a structure acting primarily in compression. However, when we remember that a **prestressed cable** is capable of sustaining compression the concept seems less absurd.

A cable dome is a spatial extension of a *Cable truss*. A cable truss is a **prestressed** truss in which the chords are tendons (straight cables) prestressed against the compression web members (often vertical). An external anchorage, or an intermediate compression chord (serving only for prestress), is needed. The structure is geometrically deformable. In the planar form this structure is rarely encountered.

A cable dome is, from the geometric viewpoint, a rib-type dome (11.7.1) in which the ribs, which are usually in compression, are replaced by prestressed cables.

For the purpose of understanding the action of the dome, it is convenient to consider it as consisting of a series of pretensioned rings with decreasing diameters (starting with the perimeter). Each set of rings consists of two rings – upper and lower – separated by compression bars.

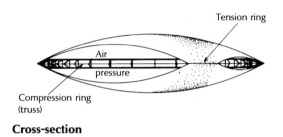

Cross-section

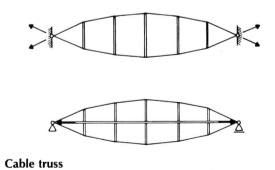

Cable truss

Each such ring is connected to the top of the outer ring (the ring of larger diameter) by diagonal cables in vertical planes. These cables form the 'ribs' of the dome.

Assuming the outer ring is stable, the set of inner rings, struts and diagonal cables can be prestressed with the outer ring forming a compression ring and the inner ring being a tension ring (see 12.2.4 above).

The outermost ring is anchored to the **edge ring** which is a stiff compression ring collecting the prestress from all the inner rings. As discussed above this compression ring is not sensitive to buckling (12.2.4).

> The whole assembly can be viewed as a series of nested bicycle wheels. The outermost wheel is very similar to a proper bicycle wheel, with the compression ring serving as the rim, and the inner pair of rings with the *struts* separating them serving as the shaft. Now, the shaft of any wheel serves as the rim of the wheel nested inside it. (It can do so by virtue of it being prestressed, allowing it to sustain compression.)

The cable dome is geometrically deformable (unlike braced domes) and is covered by a tensioned fabric membrane.

12.5 Tensegrity structures

All tension structures reviewed so far, with the exception of high pressure pneumatics, can be said to be 'externally prestressed', in the sense that the tension in the surface formed by the cable network or the fabric requires anchoring at the boundary or outside the surface.

The structures discussed in this section are **Internally prestressed cable networks**. They are prestressed, pin-jointed structures, which do not require any external anchorage. They may be considered prestressed cable networks only in the structural sense of their analysis and behaviour.

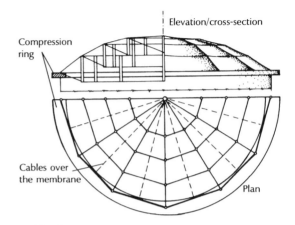

Cable dome

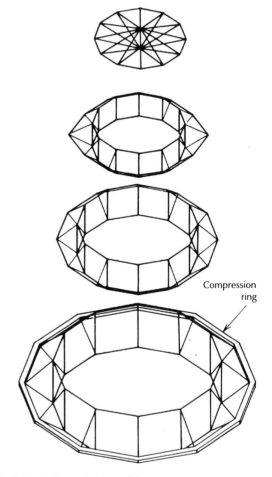

Exploded view of ring cable trusses (bicycle wheels)

Geometrically, these structures are a rather complex network of tendons (straight cables) and *Struts*. A strut is a bar, prestressed in compression. In most of the configurations proposed to date, the network of struts is disjointed, so that any strut is connected to several cables but to no other strut.

The term *Tensegrity* was coined by R. Buckminster Fuller, who was one of the pioneering proponents of this type of structure as an engineering structure. The word stands for 'tensile integrity', indicating the continuity of the cable network as opposed to the disjointed nature of the strut network. It fails however to identify the essential structural property of the system. D.G. Emmerich, another pioneer in the field, called them 'structures autotendant' or 'autotendue', namely 'self tensioned (or tensioning) structures', which is less catchy, but closer to the structural essence.

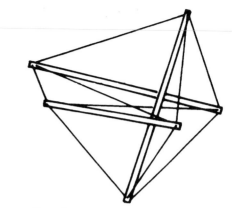

Tensegrity prism

12.5.1 Structural characterisation

The cable network is prestressed 'against' the struts, with no external anchorage required. The network as a whole is free standing. Prestress can be achieved, for instance, by lengthening the struts, thus inducing tension in the cables (through a telescoping arrangement or by extension bolts).

It is possible to view the system as though the external anchoring system, e.g. boundary elements, has been 'broken down' into short bits and 'pushed' inside the network.

There is some analogy to high pressure pneumatic structures – the air pressure has been replaced by compressed bars, but the bars do not fill the space under the cable network and instead are interlaced with it.

Single layer, double layer (the reference is to layers of cables), space filling and 'free form' configurations have been proposed. Single layer configurations require a surface of double curvature (synclastic or anticlastic), in order to avoid

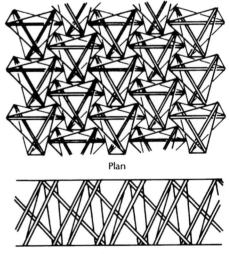

Plan

Elevation

Double-layer tensegrity grid constructed of tensegrity prisms

collision of struts (Fuller proposed domes). Double layer configurations can take any surface geometry.

The main structural problem is buckling of the highly compressed struts. In all configurations proposed to date, struts are, generally, longer than tendons – an unfavourable feature. The light appearance created by the disjointed nature of the bars is therefore misleading. Studies show that the disjointed strut configurations are generally heavier (less efficient) than bar structures of similar general layout.

To date, the only 'structures' actually constructed are free form decorative objects (sculptures, monuments), most notably by the artist Kenneth Snelson. The decorative appeal is due to the eerie appearance of the disjointed struts which appear to float in the air. It is because of their exotic appearance, as well as their convenient implementation as deployable structures, that these structures may find some limited, but highly visible scope for future applications.

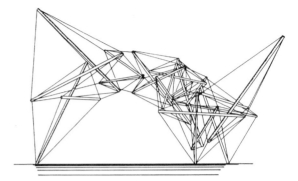

'Free ride home'

Snelson's tensegrity sculpture

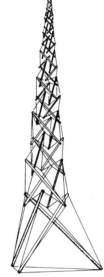

Needle tower

Geometry	Action mode	
	Direct	**Flexure**
Discrete	**Cable net**	**Boundary elements**
Continuous		**None**

Further Reading

General

Basic level

Descriptive, no mathematics:

Hilson, Barry (1993) *Basic Structural Behaviour; Understanding Structures from Models.* Thomas Telford, London.

Morgan, William (1977) *The Elements of Structures; An Introduction to the Principles of Building and Structural Engineering*, 2nd edn, SI units, (ed. I.G. Buckle). Pitman, London.

Salvadori, Mario G. & Heller, Robert (1986) *Structure in Architecture; The Building of Buildings*, 3rd. edn. Prentice-Hall, Englewood Cliffs, NJ.

Intermediate level

Level and scope approximately similar to this book:

Cowan, Henry J. & Wilson, Forrest (1981) *Structural Systems.* Van Nostrand Reinhold, New York.

Advanced level

Similar scope to this book but with a more detailed, higher computational level:

Benjamin, B.S. (1984) *Structures for Architects*, 2nd edn. Van Nostrand Reinhold, New York.

Coleman, Robert A. (1983) *Structural System Design.* Prentice-Hall, Englewood Cliffs, NJ.

Cowan, Henry J. (1980) *Architectural Structures; An Introduction to Structural Mechanics*, 1st metric edn. Pitman, London.

Lin, Tung-Yen & Stotesbury, Sydney D. (1988) *Structural Concepts and Systems for Architects and Engineers*, 2nd edn. Van Nostrand Reinhold, New York.

Salvadori, Mario G. & Levy, Matthys (1988) *Structural Design in Architecture with Examples and Problem Solutions*, 2nd edn. Prentice-Hall, Englewood Cliffs, NJ.

Schodek, Daniel L. (1992) *Structures*, 2nd edn. Prentice-Hall, Englewood Cliffs, NJ.

Schueller, Wolfgang (1996) *The Design of Building Structures.* Prentice-Hall, Upper Saddle River, NJ.

Basic structural mechanics and design of simple structures

Narrower scope, more detailed, higher computational level:

Brohn, David (1984) *Understanding Structural Analysis.* Granada, London.

Gauld, Brian J.B. (1995) *Structures for Architects*, 3rd edn. Longman Scientific & Technical, Harlow.

Nash, Alec (1990) *Structural Design for Architects.* Gower Technical, Aldershot.

Salvadori, Mario G. (1971) *Statics and Strength of Structures.* Prentice-Hall, Englewood Cliffs, NJ.

Seward, Derek (1994) *Understanding Structures; Analysis, Materials, Design.* Macmillan, Basingstoke.

Shaefer, R.E. (1993) *Elementary Structures for Architects and Builders*, 2nd edn. Prentice-Hall, Englewood Cliffs, NJ.

Specific structural systems

Steel structures

Eggen, Arne P. & Sandaker, Bjørn N. (1995) *Steel, Structure and Architecture* (translation of *Stahl, Structur og Arkitektur*). Whitney Library of Design, New York.

Shells

Faber, Colin (1963) *Candela, The Shell Builder*. Reinhold, New York.

Hennicke, Jürgen, Matsushita, Kazunori, Otto, Frei, *et al.* (eds) (1974) *Grid Shells (Gitterschalen)*. Report on the Japanese–German Research Project STI, Publication IL10. Institut für leichte Flächentragwerke (Institute for Lightweight Structures), Stuttgart. (In English, German and Japanese.)

Jödicke, Jürgen (1963) *Shell Architecture*. Reinhold, New York.

Melarango, M. (1991) *An Introduction to Shell Structures*. Van Nostrand Reinhold, New York.

Tension structures

Drew, Philip (1976) *Frei Otto – Form and Structure*. Crosby Lockwood Staples, London.

Herzog, Thomas (1977) *Pneumatic Structures; A Handbook for the Architect and Engineer*. Crosby, Lockwood Staples, London.

Otto, Frei (ed.) (1973) *Tensile Structures*. MIT Press, Cambridge, Mass.

Several publications of the Institut für leichte Flächentragwerke (Institute for Lightweight Structures, IL), Stuttgart, under the direction of Frei, Otto.

Tall buildings and towers

Billington, David P. & Goldsmith, Myron (1986) *Technique and Aesthetics in the Design of Tall Buildings*. Proceedings of the Fazlur R. Khan Memorial Session on Structural Expression in Buildings. Institute for the Study of the Highrise Habitat, Lehigh University, Bethlehem.

Heinle, Erwin (1988) *Türme aller Zeiten, aller Kulturen*. Deutsche Verlag-Anstalt, Stuttgart.

Schueller, Wolfgang (1990) *The Vertical Building Structure*. Van Nostrand Reinhold, New York.

Bridges

Billington, David P. (1990) *Robert Maillart and the Art of Reinforced Concrete*. The Architectural History Foundation, New York.

Calatrava, Santiago (1990) *Santiago Calatrava: Engineer-Architect*. Birkhäuser Verlag, Basel.

Leonhardt, Fritz (1982) *Bridges (Brücken), Aesthetics and Design*. Deutsche Verlag-Anstalt, Stuttgart.

References for structures

1. Tonon, O.L. (1993) 'Geometry of the Spatial Folded Forms', in *Space Structures 4*, Proc. 4th Intnl Conf. on Space Structures, University of Surrey, 5–10 Sept. 1993, Vol. 2, (eds G.A.R. Parkes & C.M. Howard), Thomas Telford, London.

2. Burt, M. (1996) 'Infinite Polyhedra Lattice (IPL) Space Trusses: Morphology, Analysis and Application', in *Intnl J. Space Structures* (Special issue on Morphology and Architecture), **11** (ed. H. Lalvani), pp. 115–26.

3. Gabriel, J.F. (1977) 'Are Space Frames Habitable?', in *Beyond the Cube, The Architecture of Space Frames and Polyhedra*, (ed. J.F. Gabriel), John Wiley, New York.

4. Wester, T., *Structural Order in Space, The Plate-Lattice Dualism*, Royal Academy of Arts, School of Architecture, Copenhagen.

5. Wester, T. (1996) '3-D Form and Force Language: Proposal for a Structural Basis', in *Intnl J. Space Structures*, (Special issue in Morphology and Architecture), **11** (ed. H. Lalvani), pp. 221–32.

Index of Keywords